MAN AT THE TOP

MAN AT THE TOP

Creative Leadership

RICHARD WOLFF

Tyndale House Publishers
Wheaton, Illinois

Coverdale House Publishers Ltd.
London and Eastbourne, England

Distributed in Canada by
Home Evangel Books Ltd.
Toronto, Ontario

Second printing, August 1970

Library of Congress Card Catalog No. 75-79468

Wheaton, Illinois 60187
Printed in U.S.A.

Foreword

Leadership is an art as well as a science. It is not something to to be denigrated as though it were unspiritual and worldly. Scripture is filled with illustrations of men who were leaders: Moses, Joseph, David, Isaiah, Paul. God places no premium on mediocrity and while He can and does use the weak and despised things of the world to confound the mighty, He also used and continues to use men and women of great gifts and abilities.

Men must learn to preach and teach. To this end they study and practice. The gift of leadership must also be developed by study and practice. Richard Wolff's book talks of the issue of leadership and develops the theme by way of its biblical foundations and then outlines the styles of leadership, the traits leaders need, and the cost of leadership, in addition to techniques the leader must employ in working with people. Wolff ranges widely in his sources of material and comes up with some apt illustrations and excellent and quotable material.

This is not a profound book and was not intended to be. It is popular, challenging, persuasive, and engaging. Laymen and clergy alike will be helped by reading it and using many of the suggestions it offers.

—Harold Lindsell

Table of Contents

Introduction

They were on the road, going up to Jerusalem, and Jesus was walking ahead of them; and they were amazed, and those who followed were afraid. And taking the twelve again, he began to tell them what was to happen to him . . . and James and John, the sons of Zebedee, came forward to him and said to him, "Teacher, we want you to do for us whatever we ask of you." And he said to them, "What do you want me to do for you?" And they said to him, "Grant us to sit, one at your right hand and one at your left, in your glory." But Jesus said to them, " . . . to sit at my right hand or at my left is not mine to grant, but it is for those for whom it has been prepared." And when the ten heard it, they began to be indignant at James and John. And Jesus called them to him and said to them, "You know that those who are supposed to rule over the Gentiles lord it over them, and their great men exercise authority over them. But it shall not be so among you; but whoever would be great among you must be your servant, and whoever would be first among you must be slave of all. For the Son of man also came not to be served but to serve, and to give his life as a ransom for many."

Mark 10:32-45

1

Leaders are Needed

Our generation is facing a leadership crisis. In the judgment of Karl Jaspers, "The power of leadership appears to be declining everywhere. More and more of the men we see coming to the top seem to be merely drifting."[1] The same conclusion is reached by other authors who speak of ersatz leadership or pseudo-leadership, and agree with Jaspers that "the result is helplessness in a collective leadership that hides from the public."[2]

In an ancient parable, Plato describes the following situation aboard a ship: "The captain is larger and stronger than any of the crew, but a bit deaf and shortsighted, and doesn't know much about navigation. The crew are all quarreling with each other about how to navigate the ship, each thinking he ought to be at the helm; they know no navigation and cannot say that anyone ever taught them, or that they spent any time studying it; indeed, they say it can't be taught and are ready to murder anyone who says it can. They spend all their time milling around the captain and trying to get him to give them the wheel . . . they reserve their admiration for the man who knows how to lend a hand in controlling the captain by force or fraud; they praise his seamanship and navigation and knowledge of the sea and condemn

[1]Karl Jaspers, *The Future of Mankind* (Chicago, Ill., The University of Chicago Press), 1963, p. 65.
[2]*Ibid.*

everyone else as useless. They have no idea that the true navigator must study the seasons of the year, the sky, the stars, the winds, and other professional subjects, if he is to be really fit to control a ship; and they think that it's quite impossible to acquire professional skill in navigation and that there's no such thing as an art of navigation. In these circumstances aren't the sailors on any such ship bound to regard the true navigator as a gossip and a star-gazer, of no use to them at all?"

The parable illustrates the attitude of Plato's contemporaries toward the philosopher who was the paramount leader of his day. Much the same viewpoint prevails in our own society. Under the circumstances, concludes Plato, the best philosophers are of no use to their fellowmen but the blame falls on those who fail to make use of them. Indeed, "The true and natural order is for the sick man, whether rich or poor, to wait on the doctor, and for those in need of guidance to wait on him who can give it, if he's really any use, and not for him to wait on them. And you won't be far wrong if you compare the politicians who at present rule us, to the sailors in our illustration, and those whom they call useless visionaries to the true navigators."[3]

Written four centuries before Christ, these words adequately describe the contemporary situation. Leadership is indeed lacking and the ship is adrift. Many are willing to seize the helm, but without training, without experience, without knowledge, and without confidence in the possibility of acquiring the art of leadership or navigation which is indispensable for the safety of the boat and the success of the voyage.

The success or failure, the rise and fall of groups and organizations, be they religious or secular, is determined by the quality of leadership. The need for leadership is imperative. It is therefore essential to have a clear concept of the nature of leadership. Is the personality of the leader the key to success, or is it more important to focus attention on the group? Is it possible to formulate a Christian concept of leadership? Is a certain style of leadership more likely to express scriptural concepts? Is it possible to discover potential leaders? Is leadership an art or can it be

---

[3]Plato, *The Republic* (Baltimore, Md., Penguin Books), 1963, p. 249, ff.

taught? Leadership ranges from Aaron to Zwingli. It can be exercised in many different spheres, including intellectual, economical, political, military, social, religious or artistic. From gang leader to chief executive and from pre-school teacher to university professor, leadership relates to every aspect of human endeavor. From the choir leader who directs volunteers to the five-star general who leads armies into battle, everyone is concerned with style, philosophy, and purpose of leadership. Is leadership an individual achievement, an innate ability, or a group function?

Since we hope to see strong indigenous churches come into being everywhere, we cannot ignore that such churches will not thrive without adequate indigenous leadership. What is being done to discover and train potential leaders? Can this be done? Must a specific view of Christian leadership be inculcated? Will it automatically be related to democratic concepts current in the United States? Are these concepts the most accurate reflection of a biblical style of leadership?

Broader questions perhaps should be raised. Is it legitimate for a Christian to seek leadership? Does it run counter to humility? Is ambition laudable? Should the desire to become a leader be encouraged? Is it a sign of pride? What is the relationship between the leader, the group and the historic situation?

This book will deal primarily with the person of the leader. Redemption through a person accents the biblical conviction that history as a whole must be construed through persons, not through movements or patterns. In our day it is especially necessary to stress the personality of the leader, because for too many anonymity is the saving virtue, numerical superiority the decisive consideration, and mass opinion a criterion of truth. No one cares to act in a distinctive way, since such conduct would count for nothing, except as a sign of queerness. The Christian leader should be able to speak the perceptive word which is not given to the group, the crowd, or to society as a whole. Could it be that modern studies have focused on the group and on the situation in an unconscious desire to do away with individual responsibility? Such theories may be more comfortable and convenient in an age of crisis and disillusion when the foundations crack and the edifice is tottering. A decade ago Arthur M.

Schlesinger, Jr. expressed the conviction that "whenever a society, in flight from hero worship, decides to do without great men at all, it gets into troubles of its own. Our contemporary American society, for example, has little use of the individualist. Individualism implies dissent from the group; dissent implies conflict; and conflict suddenly seems divisive, un-American, and generally unbearable. Our greatest new industry is evidently the production of techniques to eliminate conflict, from positive thoughts through public relations to psychoanalysis, applied everywhere from the couch to the pulpit. Our national aspiration has become peace of mind, peace of soul. The symptomatic drug of our age is the tranquilizer. 'Togetherness' is the banner under which we march into the brave world."[4]

Do great men shape history or are they the product of history? Does the leader create the situation, or does he emerge out of a given situation? Is leadership made possible by a coincidence between the appearance of a leader on the scene of history at the very moment when the situation demanded his particular talents? Sargent Shriver wrote, "The key to Kennedy's power is that several qualities came together in a single person at one time when the world was hungry for those qualities."[5] Can a potentially great leader not find acceptance and die unknown because the tide of history had not yet moved in his direction? Why was Luther effective whereas John Hus failed to trigger a mass movement? Jesus was not recognized by the majority of his contemporaries as a great leader. This may be our problem. The dearth of leadership may be due to our blindness.

Jesus was the leader par excellence, and it would be most surprising if, in the course of his ministry, he had not communicated some basic concepts regarding Christian leadership. This will be brought into sharp focus with the hope that it will encourage a renewal of redemptive Christian leadership.

---

[4]Arthur Schlesinger, "Greatness" *Saturday Evening Post,* Nov. 1, 1958.
[5]Sargent Shriver, *Point of the Lance* (New York, Harper & Row), 1963, p. 38.

2

Are You Qualified?

On his way to Jerusalem Jesus walked ahead of his disciples and of the crowd. This graphic picture of the order in which the Master and his disciples were traveling illustrates true leadership. The leader walks ahead of the group.

Isaiah had proclaimed that the Messiah would be "a leader and commander for the peoples" (55:4), and the New Testament stresses the obvious fulfillment. Jesus Christ is declared to be the *Leader* and Savior, the Pioneer of our faith and of our salvation, and the *Author* of life (Acts 3:15, 5:31; Heb. 2:10, 12:2). In these passages the same Greek word is translated Leader, Pioneer, and Author. Originally it described the *hero* of a city or the founding father who gave his name to the city. For instance, Alexandria in Egypt was founded by Alexander the Great. The *hero* was the originator or the author. He had the primacy in terms of time and power in terms of rank. He was the captain, the political or military leader marching at the head of a company as leader and guide. The nuances of this Greek term justify different translations of the word in the New Testament. Author and originator, chief leader and prince, forerunner and model—all these aspects are involved.

The leader is the first to do or to accomplish anything. He precedes, guides by going in advance—Jesus was walking ahead of the disciples in the true fashion of a leader. When Israel left Egypt God *went before* them day and night in order to *lead them*

(Ex. 13:21). Moses prayed that after his death God would "appoint a man over the congregation, who shall *go* out *before* them and come in before them, who shall *lead* them out and bring them in; that the congregation of the Lord may not be as sheep who have no shepherd" (Num. 27:17). Jesus spoke of the shepherd who *goes before* the sheep (Jn. 10:4). In all these biblical passages the concept of leadership is intimately related to the idea of "going before." Leadership implies precedence, linked with the idea of capacity for drawing others, or fitness to guide them.

The simplest description of a leader is that he is walking ahead of the group. He keeps in advance without completely detaching himself from the crowd. He influences his followers and moves them toward desirable goals.

The word "leadership" has been used as an omnibus term, indiscriminately applied to the playground supervisor and the business executive. It is not difficult to recognize the difference between manager and prophet, partisan leader and saint, autocratic and democratic leader, paternalist and expert.

There are many areas and styles of leadership, but all of them involve, in varying degrees, a walking ahead of the group. As John Mott, himself a dynamic leader, expressed it: "A leader is a man who knows the road, who can keep ahead, and who can pull others after him."[1]

Some leaders have achieved preeminence because of unique attainments, others have received leadership status by official designation, and a few have emerged as leaders in a crisis situation. Regardless of how the leadership position was reached, or what style of leadership was adopted, the broad definition—that a leader walks ahead of the group, exercising influence on the group—holds true.

Jesus walked ahead of the disciples. A study of leadership cannot ignore the disciples, the followers, the group. If the leader walks ahead of the crowd, then the very word "leader" implies followers, as well as a relationship between the leader and the followers. Finally, both the leader and the group have to be seen in a specific environment. It is imperative to be conscious of these

---

[1]As quoted by J. Oswald Sanders, *Spiritual Leadership* (Chicago, Ill., Moody Press), 1967, p. 19.

four elements: the leader, the followers, their relationship, and the environment or situation.

In the biblical passage quoted on the first page of this book, the situation is graphically described. James and John come forward with an ambitious request: "Grant us to sit, one at your right hand and one at your left, in your glory." Jesus' answer is most remarkable. He does not condemn ambition per se, but says: "To sit at my right hand or at my left is not mine to grant, but is for those for whom it has been prepared." Dignity is not conferred on the basis of arbitrary selection. Did he mean to tell them that the prerogative of dispensing those glories was not his, but another's? Surely not; for the Son of man will dispense them as the Judge at the last day. Did he mean to say that he had no authority of his own to give away the glories of heaven? Surely not; for there is given to him authority: "All judgment is committed to him, because he is the Son of man." But the plain meaning was that they were not his to give by absolute or arbitrary right.

According to Jesus, greatness must be earned. The steps to glory are not won by favoritism. The kingdom of God is not like the kingdoms of the world. Of course, even a secular state is unusually corrupt and unwholesome when places of high distinction can be obtained by solicitation rather than on the basis of fitness. If such a procedure is inadmissable in any well-regulated secular state, how preposterous to think that promotion by favoritism can take place in the kingdom of God.

If the ten were indignant at James and John and felt so keenly the wrong done, it was because they were animated by the same spirit and cherished the same ambitions. Each of the ten was looking forward to his throne, and several wished to be regarded as the greatest. Jesus took advantage of this situation to instruct the Apostles regarding leadership and greatness. He immediately rejected the thought of partiality and patronage and sketched a sharp contrast between his kingdom and the kingdoms of the earth, especially regarding the acquisition of preeminence. "You know that those who are supposed to rule over the Gentiles lord it over them, that their great men exercise authority over them." The words "you know" indicate that Jesus Christ spoke of things as they were at the time, especially in the Roman Empire. Imperial power was founded on conquest, authority was based on might, the great were the strong. The rulers used tyrannical power and oppressive despotism.

But the contrast is evident not only in the manner of using power but in the way of acquiring it: "Whoever would be great among you must be your servant, and whoever would be first among you must be slave of all." Some "would be great." Jesus recognized the existence of a desire to greatness, an aspiration to leadership, an ambition to preeminence and does *not* condemn it. He juxtaposes such terms as "great" and "servant," "first" and "slave," "greatest" and "youngest," the "leader" and the "one who serves" (cf. Lk. 22:26). The desire to lead exists and is legitimate. "The point on which he wishes to fix the attention of his disciples is the peculiar way he takes to get his crown; and what he says in effect is this: 'I am a king, and I expect to have a kingdom; James and John were not mistaken in that respect. But I shall obtain my kingdom in another way than secular princes get theirs. They get their thrones by succession, I get mine by personal merit; they secure their kingdom by right of birth, I hope to secure mine by right of service; they inherit their subjects, I buy mine, the purchase money being mine own life.' "[2]

Christ indicates a new direction and presses upon his disciples the necessity of qualifying for the duties of true leadership. Greatness is not related to possessions—the Son of man had no place to lay his head. Greatness is not determined by power. Despotic rule is tyrannical and results in bondage. True Christian leadership is redemptive and results in freedom. The full implication of these words will gradually unfold. Some basic presuppositions must first be stated and potential roadblocks removed. The role of ambition in Christian service needs clarification.

---

[2]A. B. Bruce, *The Training of the Twelve* (Garden City, New York, Doubleday, Doran & Co.), 1928, pp. 281–296.

3

Is It Right To Be Ambitious?

Peer Gynt, the hero of one of Ibsen's plays, was driven by restless ambition. Ibsen describes the struggle between the divine purpose and human passions. Peer Gynt hoped to achieve something really big, to become king or emperor. He saw himself at the head of a mighty army; his horse had a crest of shining silver and four shoes of gold, and Peer Gynt exclaimed: "I can do anything." Convulsively he asserts his individuality and demands absolute sway. He dreams of a city called *Peer*opolis and of a new land called *Gynt*iana, but his imaginary freedom is empty, purposeless, and his ambition pointless. He is an emperor *manqué,* missing the divine purpose for his life. This tragic picture of misguided ambition evokes by contrast the image of legitimate aspiration.

Not everyone may be called to be a shining button on the waistcoat of the world, but it is important to emphasize the legitimacy of ambition, of the desire to be a leader. Christ speaks of some who will be great, will be first, will be leaders. Paul praises the man who aspires to the office of bishop, who *desires* a noble task (I Tim. 3:1). Paul commends such an ambition. The word he uses really means to stretch out in order to touch or grasp something; to reach after, or desire something. Such ambition is noble—and necessary. Without such keen desire the burden of leadership will not be assumed; the risk is too great, the cost too high, the work too arduous and the responsibility too heavy.

Paul speaks of his own ambition to preach the Gospel.* Paul does not hesitate to say: I have reason to be proud of my work for God (Romans 15:17). Robert Haldane comments with remarkable insight: "This shows that although all success is of God, yet it is an honor and a ground of praise to be successful in Christ's work. Many have supposed that it is wrong to give any praise to God's servants on account of their labors, diligence, and success in his service. They have judged that this encourages a spirit of self-righteousness and of pride. But the wisdom is not from God. It is human wisdom, and tends to dampen exertion in the service of Jesus Christ. All our success is in Jesus Christ, as well as our ability and disposition to labor. Yet God has given praise to his servants for their diligence and success in his work. It is a sinful refinement to blame what God approves."[1] To the Romans Paul mentions his ambition, his aspiration to preach the gospel where the gospel of Christ had not yet been proclaimed. Such ambition is lawful and commendable in any Christian.

In order to do the will of God it is essential for each man to know his divinely-appointed sphere and limit (II Cor. 10:8-18), to use the gifts which he has received, to be a faithful steward, to trade with his talents, to recognize and to accept his God-given role, i.e. to shoulder his responsibility and to accomplish his task. Such ambition is not only legitimate, but a necessary ingredient of leadership. Christian ambition rises on the basis of talents received. It is a response to the call to faithfulness, to the divine challenge. It is expressed in a willingness to lead, to accept the summons to greatness, i.e. to redemptive service.

Every virtue has been counterfeited, and ambition is no exception. There are always those who tell you how good they are; "their trouble is that they are only comparing themselves with each other and measuring themselves against their own little

---

*Romans 15:20: literally, the Greek word translated "ambition" means "love of honor."

[1]Robert Haldane, *The Epistle to the Romans* (London, The Banner of Truth Trust), 1958, Comm. on 15:20.

ideas" (II Cor. 10:12—*Living Letters*). Diotrephes is a prime example of misguided ambition. He liked to put himself first, refused to welcome the brethren, stopped those who wanted to welcome them, and put them out of the church (III Jn. 9-11). Proud Diotrephes loved to push himself forward as the leader of the Christians, seeking preeminence and not admitting any other authority. Christian ambition does not run counter to true humility.

Moses was one of the great leaders of Israel. At the age of forty he hoped to deliver his people, but they did not understand that God had chosen him for this task (Acts 7:23-25). The question was raised: Who made you a ruler and a judge over us? Moses carried this question with him into the wilderness and after forty years returned with the answer. He never lost sight of his ambitious task, but maintained the burning desire to liberate his people. His ambition had been right, but his methodology had been wrong. God used him at the age of eighty.

Persistent desire and ambition has always characterized the true leader. According to the historian Morison, Ulysses S. Grant "was unfitted for the Presidency by temperament, and less equipped for it than any predecessor or successor."[2] He disliked war, loathed army routine, and was ultimately forced to resign from the army to avoid a court martial for drunkenness. He attempted to sell real estate but failed. After the close of his Presidency his income was insufficient for the proper support of his family. He invested all of his available property in a banking house, but paid no attention to the management of the business. He soon became bankrupt. Misfortune was balanced by heroism. Although he suffered from cancer of the throat, he finished his *Personal Memoirs* four days before his death.

How did Ulysses Grant reach the highest office in the land? By his own account, as a West Point cadet Grant was more stirred by the commanding appearance of General Winfield Scott than by any man he had ever seen, including the President. He wrote that when he saw General Scott, the thought flashed

---

[2]Samuel Eliot Morison, *The Oxford History of the American People* (New York, Oxford University Press), 1965, p. 726.

across his mind, that someday he would stand in Scott's place. The desire was kindled and maintained throughout the subsequent career of U.S. Grant.

Only those who have a genuine desire for leadership will be sufficiently motivated to shoulder the responsibilities implicit in the task. When young Benjamin Disraeli attended Parliament he began at once to dream of becoming a statesman. He imagined himself speaking to Parliament with irresistible arguments, with flashes of wit, floods of humor, and compelling peroration. He was defeated repeatedly before gaining a seat in the House of Commons and his maiden speech was a failure. He was laughed down, but only after he warned his interrupters that one day they would have to listen to him.

One of the strangest prayers in Scripture is the ambitious request of Jabez, who called upon the God of Israel and asked for enlargement of his territory, success in his ventures and security against foes. God granted what he asked (I Chron. 4:10). It is true that ambition can be rooted in supreme selfishness. It can be motivated by ego-expression or hunger for power. It can spring from a desire to gain recognition or significance.

True Christian ambition was not condemned by Jesus, who reminded the disciples: If any man *desire* to be first, he must be last of all and servant of all (Mk. 9:35). The intention of the Master was not to enact a penal provision against seeking the mastery, but to point out the way to true greatness through humility and service. It is highly significant that the desire to be great is associated with the concept of humility and the idea of service.

The idea that a true and safe leader is likely to be one who has no desire to lead, or the belief that the man who is ambitious to lead is disqualified as a leader, runs counter to Scripture and experience. Noble and worthy ambitions should be cultivated, and the desire to be a Christian leader should be encouraged.

4

Can A Leader Be Humble?

Legitimate ambition, the desire to be a leader, does not run counter to true humility. Paul's admonition, "In humility count others better than yourselves" (Phil. 2:3), does not abolish the concept of leadership. This verse will be fulfilled with "logic true to the soul, when each sees himself, the personality he knows best, in the light of eternal holiness."[1] The comment by Timothy Dwight is significant: "This precept, which to a man of the world appears absurd and incapable of being obeyed, involves no difficulty in the eye of him who is evangelically humble. The sins of other Christians are, of course, imperfectly known to him. Their sins of thought are all hidden from his eyes; their sins of action he rarely witnesses; and of those which are perpetrated in his presence, he cannot know either the extent or malignity. His own sins, in the meantime, both of heart and of life, are in a sense always naked before him; and he can hardly fail to discern, in some good degree, their number, their aggravations and their guilt. Hence other Christians will, in a comparative sense, appear to him to be clean; while himself will seem unsound and polluted, from the crown of the head to the sole of the foot. In this situation, the difficulty of esteeming others better than himself vanishes. Impossible as it

[1]H.C.G. Moule, *Philippian Studies* (London, Hodder & Stoughton), 1900, *in loco*.

would be for the proud man to think in this manner, the only difficulty to the humble man is to think in any other."[2]

Mention has already been made of Moses and of his desire to be the leader and liberator of his nation. He was elevated above all the elders of the nation, but his superiority did not conflict with his meekness and humility.

The man Moses was very meek, more than all men that were on the face of the earth (Num. 12:3). This character trait is mentioned in a significant context where doubt might have arisen about his humility. Ambition and humility did not exclude each other.

Evangelical humility is based on and conformed to the real circumstances and character of man. The views which the humble man entertains of himself and of his condition are an exact reflection of his situation. The humble estimate is the true one. He is just such a person as he supposes himself to be and in just such a condition. His views about himself are true and therefore humble, lowly.

Modesty denotes the absence of *undue* self-confidence and may adequately reflect the biblical concept of humility. This attitude should not be confused with shyness or timidity. True humility is not depicted in this funeral eulogy pronounced by a priest at the graveside: "He was not wealthy, neither was he clever: his bearing was unmanly, his voice weak, uncertain in expressing an opinion. He scarce seemed master even in his home. He slunk into church as though he sought to beg permission to take his place with all the rest . . . Where'er he went, he seemed to dread being seen."[3]

Christ made the extraordinary claim: no one knows the Father except the Son. The immediate context speaks of his humility (Matt. 11:25-30). These claims are not contradictory. Humility is to confess our true condition. Christ as the Son of God made this unique claim in all humility. For fallen man, humility always involves the admission of sin because it is part of our true condition.

Christ and the Scriptures make room for legitimate ambition. Some received more talents than others, each one according to his ability; each one was responsible to trade with the pounds he re-

---

[2]Timothy Dwight, *Theology* (Middletown, Conn.), 1818, Vol. III, p. 364.
[3]Henrick Ibsen, *Peer Gynt* (Garden City, N.Y., Doubleday & Co., Inc.), 1963, Act. V.

ceived. God has given to each of us the ability to do certain things well. Each member of the body has a specific function and has been placed by God where he wants it.

The earth trembles when a slave becomes king because it is not fitting for a slave to rule over princes (Prov. 30:21, 22 and 19:10). It was one of the judgments announced by Isaiah that God would place boys in position of authority and that babes should rule over Israel (Isa. 3:4). It was inconceivable to have a slave or a boy on the throne of Israel. The situation would have been abnormal and the arrangement of society shattered. Seldom will the slave who has been freed be able to rise above the limited level of his earlier state.

General Ambrose E. Burnside had been successful in small military operations. But, "it is not unusual in war for an officer, competent on one echelon, to be a failure on the next one higher. The captain of a battleship may prove to be incapable of handling a task-force, a division commander may be no good when placed over an army corps, and so on. Burnside, to do him justice, didn't want the new command, felt inadequate; but he went in and did his best, which unfortunately was very bad indeed."[4] It remains true in every sphere of life that in his divine sovereignty God has distributed gifts to each one according to his ability.

Jesus did not have to admonish the Twelve to be ambitious, but too often their desires and aspirations moved in the wrong direction. They were leaders, chosen for a purpose, and Jesus trained them in the art of true leadership: If anyone would be first, he must be last of all and servant of all . . . whoever would be great among you must be your servant, and whoever would be first among you must be slave of all (Mk. 9:35; 10:43, 44).

A false concept of humility will inhibit creativity and stifle initiative. Not humiliation and external submission to God nor annihilation of the human will, but the creative realization of the will of God is the call of God. Humility is an escape from one's hardened selfhood and the asphyxiating atmosphere of one's own limited self. Humility is an expression of freedom because no one in the world can force humility upon us. The slavish, external interpretation of humility is foreign to the spirit of the gospel. Am-

[4]Samuel Eliot Morison, *op. cit.*, p. 655.

bition and humility are not mutually exclusive. Ambition does not disqualify nor humility exclude from Christian leadership. Both are necessary.

Paul did not hesitate to write that he had worked harder than any of the other Apostles because of his ambition to plant churches in areas where Christ had not yet been proclaimed. Conscious of his achievements he knew that God's grace towards him had not been in vain. At the same time he recognized: "It was not I, but the grace of God which is with me" (I Cor. 15:10). Notice the words *with me*, i.e. in efficient fellowship with me. H.A.W. Meyer comments, "Paul does not disclaim for himself his own self-active share in bringing about the result, but knows that the intervention of divine grace so *outweighs* his own activity, that to the alternative, whether he or grace has wrought such great things, he can only answer as he has done: *not I, but the grace of God with me.*"[5] Paul acknowledged the preponderance of grace, but even then he wrote: "God's grace worked *with me.*" He could not disregard his own efforts or discard the word "me." Paul recognized the efficacy of God's grace, but at the same time stressed his personal activity. His was true evangelical humility.

[5]H.A.W. Meyer, *Commentary on the New Testament,* (New York, Funk & Wagnalls), 1884, *in loco.*

5

Which Style Should You Adopt?

Democratic Leadership

One of the most striking features of the twentieth century is the rapid diffusion of the idea of democracy. At this point in history most governments would insist that they are democratic, or at least striving to become so. This is also true in the area of leadership.

Originally the word "democracy" described a form of government where the right to make political decisions was exercised directly by the entire body of citizens. Subsequently this right was exercised through representatives. To a large extent, the activities of the typical democratic leader are determined by the needs of the group. The democratic leader merely defines these needs with greater precision. He is the incarnation of their collective aspirations. He sees what they see and he feels what they feel, but more sharply and in clearer focus. He contracts the crowd into the span of his own personality. He converts them into a composite second self. He is like the leader of an orchestra obtaining harmonious and melodious cooperation from all his musicians, adding to the symphonic effect the charm of his own interpretation.

Democratic leadership is characterized by group participation. Policies become matters of group discussion and decision. The role of the democratic leader is to encourage and to assist, and if he makes any suggestions at all he is sure to present several alternatives. Such a style of leadership demands that appropriate communication channels be created to inform the entire group, and that adequate time be available for discussion.

This style of leadership is possible only with a well-educated group. The problem to be discussed must be understood by the group and must be related to their problem-solving ability. Intense group participation is desirable. The democratic style of leadership presupposes a highly motivated group.

Every style of leadership is subject to serious limitations. The atmosphere is not always conducive to the ideal exercise of democratic leadership. At times it seems that the only possible action is to appoint another committee—which is the thing to be done when nothing is to be done, but the illusion is maintained that action has been taken. Progress may be slow or impeded if the group lacks adequate communication, motivation, or education. Even in the best democracy it is necessary occasionally to resort to disciplinary action. This tends to become a major problem in democratic leadership because it is difficult to know how discipline should be exercised.

Sometimes, in the name of democracy, high quality is destroyed and individual greatness rejected. Quality is subject to quantity, individual to mass, genius to average.

Some members of the group want the leader to take more initiative and are uncomfortable when decision-making is shared. They are impatient with extended discussion and want to get on with the job. At the same time democratic leadership may produce higher morale and greater productivity.

The astute observation of Karl Jaspers should not be disregarded: "The politician regards public opinion as given fact and submits to it, whereas the statesman creates public opinion, seeing through the talk of the day to the hidden will, which he awakens."[1]

The danger, vastly increased by modern mass media, is to use fashionable catch words, promoting a multitude of aimless hopes and groundless fears, footless action and lost motion. The demagogue is always moving on the lowest level of the passions

---

[1]Karl Jaspers, *op. cit.*, p. 241.

of the crowd. Such a man has no lifting power, never touches the higher desires of the group, never awakens deeper concerns or considerations. We are well aware of the temptation to determine action by political consideration and to sacrifice principle to expediency in order to retain leadership.

Mao Tse-tung's views on democratic leadership are interesting. He coined the formula "from the masses to the masses" and explains:

Take the ideas of the masses (scattered and unsystematic ideas) and concentrate them (through study turn them into concentrated and systematic ideas); then go to the masses and propagate and explain these ideas until the masses embrace them as their own, hold fast to them, and translate them into action. Test the correctness of these ideas in such action. Then once again concentrate ideas from the masses and once again go to the masses so that the ideas are persevered in and carried through. And so on, over and over again in an endless spiral, with the ideas becoming more correct, more vital and richer each time. Such is the Marxist theory of knowledge . . .

The masses in any given place are generally composed of three parts, the relatively active, the intermediate, and the relatively backward. The leaders must therefore be skilled in uniting the small number of active elements around the leadership and must rely on them to raise the level of intermediate element and to win over the backward elements.[2]

Autocratic Leadership

At the very opposite pole of democratic leadership is the autocratic style. This may be most congenial to Christian leaders whose firm convictions regarding the will of God may unconsciously tend in this direction. Is it not true that the prophet was a spokesman, a representative of authority? Is it necessary to waste time in consultation when one is sure of the Divine will?

Originally, the office of the dictator was established for the purpose of meeting a military crisis. The dictator only functioned in times of emergencies arising from external threats or internal

[2]Quotations from Chairman Mao Tse-tung (N.Y., Bantam Books), 1967, p. 70–71.

frenzy. The legal symbolism of Rome required that the dictator be elected in the darkness of night. The Romans were well aware of the fact that the concentration of power in the hands of a dictator could easily lead to despotic and dictatorial rule, to autocratic and authoritative government, to totalitarianism and absolutism.

The autocratic leader seldom hesitates. He knows what should be done and never seems in doubt. He drives ahead and is often careless of human feelings. He is often the man of striking achievements. Perhaps there are times and places where autocratic leadership will provide unity of purpose and a clarity of intention for which people passionately yearn—the office was created to meet an emergency.

The word dictator evokes the memory of Caesar, Louis XIV, Genghis Khan, and Stalin. But such "outright tyranny without concern for the appearance of popular consent is the most old fashioned of political maneuvers today. The truly modern dictator achieves his goal *through* the people, not in spite of them. He rides their aspirations to power. He manipulates their hopes and fears and is ushered into office with their joyous shouts. He may then construct, with the consent of the people, precisely the same machinery of control that he would otherwise have had to construct over their opposition."[3]

The weaknesses of this type of leadership are glaring. The autocratic leader is often inflexible. If it is assumed that one rules by divine right, or if a leader is absolutely sure to work in harmony with Providence, inflexibility will inevitably result. The leader may claim that the end will be beneficial to all, but the ultimate purpose cannot be divorced from the means which are employed. If a man strives for love by means of hatred, for brotherhood by means of dissension, for truth by means of falsehood, his lofty aim is not likely to make our judgment of him more lenient.

Talleyrand once said to Napoleon: You can do everything with bayonets, Sire, except sit on them—to rule is not the gesture of snatching at power, but the tranquil exercise of it. It has sometimes been said that real statesmen are inspired by nothing

[3]John W. Gardner, *Self-Renewal* (N.Y., Harper & Row), 1965, pp. 55–56.

else than instinct for power and love of country. Napoleon possessed this craving for power along with the supreme indifference to the risk of death, whether his own or that of others. J. Christopher Herold points out that "Napoleon almost never made a decision with one single purpose in mind; in some cases his principal objective proved to be unattainable; one or several alternative courses of action remained open to him so that no effort was entirely wasted. It was this pliability of his that explains changing methods, but unchanging objectives and ultimate goals."[4]

The autocratic leader tends to forget that "without people a prince is ruined" (Prov. 14:28). Solitary splendor is self-extinguishing. When population diminishes and followers dwindle, decline sets in, because "in a multitude of people is the glory of a king."

Autocratic leadership is very common and typical of most tribal leaders. The Valiente Indians of Panama express the concept of authority by the phrase "those on the handle." The ruler is the one who has the handle of the hunting knife in his hand. Others could grasp only the blade and would be injured in the process. Only the ruler can wield the knife and control its power—a graphic picture of autocratic leadership.

It has often been said that power corrupts. It should not be overlooked that weakness, too, corrupts. "Power corrupts the few, while weakness corrupts the many. Hatred, malice, rudeness, intolerance, suspicion are the fruits of weakness. The resentment of the weak does not spring from any injustice done to them, but from the sense of inadequacy and impotence."[5]

If the behavior of the leader is to be related to the expectations of the group, then a democratic approach would fail whenever the group expects autocratic action. Style and situation cannot be divorced.

Paternalistic Leadership

Paternalistic leadership is yet another style. The identification between the leader and the group is almost complete. The leader

[4] J. Christopher Herold, *The Age of Napoleon* (N.Y., American Heritage Publishing Co.), 1963, p. 235.

[5] Eric Hoffer, *The Ordeal of Change* (N.Y., Harper & Row), 1963, pp. 11–12.

has a fatherlike attitude and is deeply concerned for the welfare of each individual group member. Whereas the autocratic leader remains aloof, the paternalistic leader identifies with the group. Such leadership is well-meaning, but weak. When the paternalistic leader disappears from the scene, the group is left helpless—just as much as when the autocratic leader is removed.

Moses was fearful of becoming a paternalistic leader and pleaded with God to give him a successor. Moses prayed that God would "appoint a man over the congregation, who shall go out before them and come in before them, who shall lead them out and bring them in; that the congregation of the Lord may not be as sheep which have no shepherd" (Num. 27:15-17). Moses did not indulge in excessive grief upon hearing that he would not lead Israel into the promised land. He did not appoint a member of his own family to succeed him. He was concerned about the nation and asked God to appoint another shepherd. Empathy on the part of the leader without corresponding initiative is merely pity.

Identification on the part of the group with those on a higher plane may degenerate into admiration and pseudo-worship. Because God is presented in the Scriptures as the Father of believers and the Good Shepherd, a paternalistic type of leadership may appeal to many Christian leaders. Such a style seems to preserve the concept of fellowship better than the democratic or autocratic method. The family atmosphere prevails. This may be very pleasant, although it can happen at the expense of efficiency. Discipline is difficult to maintain. Paternalism may degenerate into weakness because of an exaggerated identification of the leader with the group. At the other end of the spectrum it may also disguise a dictatorial approach to leadership since paternal authority and wisdom are not open to question.

Partisan Leadership

Intense concern may give birth to partisan leadership. The call to labor among Jews may lead to a disregard of all other ethnic groups. The same holds true of other exclusive preoccupations. The focus is so sharp and narrow that all else is eliminated.

The partisan leader is a man of strong convictions. He tends to minimize the weaknesses of his own group, especially if he is the "founder and director." Capable in his specific area, he is often narrow in his outlook. The intensity of his dedication to the cause tends to move the partisan leader to extremism. Zealous, crusading, single-minded, absolute,—such a leader can easily become fanatic, incapable of entertaining more than one thought. He leads a minority with unflinching courage. The ideas and interests of the group as interpreted by the leader become an all-consuming flame. He carries the torch regardless of obstacles, and glories in tribulation and martyrdom—imaginary or real. His character is granite; he moves with assurance and can accomplish much.

Indentification with a specific group tends to make one partisan and narrow. This is reflected in the partisan style of leadership. It is true that the sympathies of every leader are largely determined by his purposes, but he should never lose sight of all else. His energies and sympathies can and should be directed toward a specific group, class, nation, or race, but he should never forget mankind as a whole regardless of the intensity of his particular concern.

Laissez-Faire

This approach reduces the leadership role to the barest essentials. Minimum direction and maximum individual freedom of action is the motto.

Herbert Spencer popularized a phrase of Thomas Paine: "That government is best which governs least." Applied to the laissez-faire style of leadership it reduces the role of the leader to the establishment of a friendly, comfortable atmosphere. The policy is to give almost total freedom for group decisions, involving a minimum of leader participation. The leader recedes into the background and at times might even refuse to discuss or appraise. He establishes rapport, uses few words, accepts intervals of silence and creates a permissive atmosphere. Laissez-faire leadership is a term covering a broad spectrum, but in all its variations it reflects the same basic philosophic outlook.

The non-directive approach is based on the assumption that remedial forces exist within human nature and that these innate restorative capacities should come into play in the relationship between the leader and the group. At this point the leader is barely ahead of the group so that the concept of leadership is almost relinquished. The relationship is similar to the one between the therapist and the patient, where concern replaces direction and self-understanding takes precedence.

The Expert

Something must be said about the expert who plays such a significant role in our age of specialization. Should we follow the advice of Vergil: *Expert Credite,* believe the expert? Or is it true that the expert is the one who avoids small errors as he sweeps on to the grand fallacy?

"The best-informed man is not necessarily the wisest. Indeed there is a danger that precisely in the multiplicity of his knowledge he will lose sight of what is essential. But on the other hand, knowledge of an apparently trivial detail quite often makes it possible to see into the depths of things. And so the wise man will seek to acquire the best possible knowledge about events, but always without becoming dependent upon this knowledge."[6]

These words of Bonhoeffer indicate both the significance and the limitation of the expert. An expert may become a leader in his own field, but his achievement in one particular area does not necessarily qualify him for leadership in unrelated fields. Sometimes he tends to see his own specialty large and the rest of the world small. His analysis may not be sufficiently broad because he is tempted to see everything under a restricted and specific angle. Unless the specialist informs himself to a reasonable degree, going beyond his own narrow horizon, he can easily be mistaken in an area where his critical faculties have no familiar data on which to work. The knowledge of the expert may be limited to a tiny portion of the universe, but he may be tempted to adopt strong attitudes and to present them forcefully in areas outside of his particular specialty.

---

[6]Dietrich Bonhoeffer, *Ethics* (N.Y., Macmillan Co.), 1965, p. 69.

Under Solomon, a significant transition took place in Israel. A pastoral society was gradually being transformed into an urban society. There were few skilled workers such as carpenters and goldsmiths. Solomon faced a dilemma when he undertook to build the Temple. He brought in foreign experts. In his letter to Hiram he admitted, "There is no one among us who knows how to cut timber like the Sidonians." He invited the pagan experts to help Israel erect the Temple of God. Archeological discoveries confirm what we might have guessed—that the external features of the Temple were strikingly similar to pagan temples of the period. The style was practically identical. The difference was spiritual, internal, essential.

Solomon needed the expertise of the foreigners and used them without hesitation for a sacred task. He recognized that in spite of his wisdom—or better, he recognized because of his wisdom—that he required the knowledge of the specialist. The leader must find the expert, listen to him, grasp the essential, allow him to work and to obtain the results—without becoming a specialist himself and without ever losing sight of the whole, the overall picture.

Every task calls for a division of labor and every division of labor presupposes the unity of the whole. "Departments have a limited meaning. The whole which unites them also limits their realm of validity; it is their source and their guidepost."[7]

Solomon pursued the grand strategy, the overall plan, the ultimate goal. He used experts in a specific area. He imported Hiram, a man of Tyre "trained to work in gold, silver, bronze, iron, stone, and wood, and in purple, blue, and crimson fabrics and fine linen, and to do all sorts of engraving and *execute* any design that may be *assigned* him" (II Chron. 2:14 ff). Hiram had the necessary understanding, wisdom, and skill; Solomon formulated the plan and assigned the work, never losing sight of the grand design.

There are many other styles of leadership. Some do not depend upon face-to-face contact between leader and followers. This would be true, for instance, of intellectual and aesthetic leadership.

---

[7]Karl Jaspers, *op. cit.*, p. 9.

Many monuments have been erected to those who gained no recognition from their contemporaries. As Jesus said to the Pharisees, "You build monuments to the prophets killed by your fathers and lay flowers on the graves of the godly men they destroyed . . ." (Mt. 23:29). The artist is frequently ahead of his time and sounds a prophetic note.

The Manager

The manager, or executive, is a leader whose overall goal is largely defined and he may only be able to broaden or refine it. It has been suggested that a good manager might adopt different styles of leadership in order to match specific situations. Some may find it easier to modify the situation in order to bring it in line with their style of leadership.

More and more young people take for granted that their life will be enmeshed with a fairly large corporation. This does not necessarily imply conformity. Today's executive stresses effectiveness. "They get things done. They are task oriented. They want results—and are willing to work hard to get them."[8] The young executive is described as serious, aggressive, confident, independent, and decisive.

Management is defined as the art or science of getting things done through people.[9] Management is the art of purposeful action; it is the bringing together of ends and means, or the usage of means towards specific ends. Administration is the capacity of coordinating conflicting social energies in a single organism so adroitly that they operate as a unit.

The role of the manager is to define policies and procedures and to organize the activities of others toward a common goal. He interprets and transmits policies, but at the same time is asked to galvanize unrelatedness into group unity, stimulating and vitalizing all he touches. He is usually characterized by strong orientation and has learned the art of purposeful action.

---

[8]Walter Guzzardi Jr., *The Young Executive* (N. Y., The New American Library), 1966, p. IX.
[9]See "Management" by Wallace A. Erickson, pg. 5. This booklet is available through International Christian Broadcaster, 1111 Nicollet Avenue, Minneapolis, Minnesota, 55403. It draws valuable distinctions between the manager and the entrepreneur.

More recently some attention has been focused on the natural or emerging leader. The charismatic leader—such as the prophet—has played a significant role in history. The diplomatic leader, the arbitrator, the mediator—all function in different leadership roles.

Jesus frequently asked questions, adopting a Socratic style, acting as a catalyst. At the same time his authoritative statements were so strong that people questioned him regarding the source of his authority.

It is apparent from this brief review that every style of leadership has its peculiar advantages and pitfalls and must be evaluated against the specific situation in which leadership is exercised. It must be remembered there is no hard and fast line between different styles of leadership. A partisan leader might be democratic, paternalistic, or autocratic. Again, every type of leadership must be permissive to a certain extent, unless it is purely autocratic. Perhaps it would not be wrong to speak of a democratic-autocratic continuum, determined by the situation, the task, the personality of the leader, the nature of the group, and related factors. Other styles could be described, and many significant questions could be raised, but perhaps the central question remains: Is there a distinctive Christian concept of leadership?

6

A Christian Concept of Leadership

There is a striking contrast between the proud aristocrat pictured by Aristotle, living to prove his independence and superiority, and the life surrendered in humility and service as requested by Jesus Christ.

According to the Greek philosopher, the superior man is one who claims—and is entitled to claim—high consideration from his fellowman. The superior man is deeply concerned with honor, not, however, honor received from men lacking special qualities to recommend them! To be honored by such men is altogether beneath him. The superior man looks down on people and despises the rest of the world, because he sees himself at the center of the universe and evaluates all his relationships accordingly. This superior man despises being the recipient of benefits and has a far better memory for benefits conferred than received. In his supreme indifference he is immune to outside influence and ever reluctant to ask for help.

This picture of the superior man is diametrically opposed to that presented by Jesus Christ. He characterized the leader as one who serves and whose ministry is redemptive: "Whoever would be great among you, must be your servant." The motivation is love, the method is service, the purpose is redemption, the result is freedom.

Love—The Motive of Leadership

The love of God is at the root of the Christian life. The love *of* God, is the love which originates in God, has its source in him and of which we are the object. My love to God is only an echo, a response—not immutable but fluctuating and changeable. It is the love of Christ, his love to me, which brings molding power into my life and becomes the controlling factor, impelling, urging and constraining (II Cor. 5:14). The fact that God loves me becomes the motivating power of the Christian life. It leads to response, to service. The service Jesus requires is determined by love. "Thou shalt love *thy neighbor as thyself*." The neighbor is in view —the leader sees the group. But the accent also falls on the words *"as thyself."* Calvin observed that the Lord "in order to give us the best expression of the strength of that love which we ought to exercise toward our neighbors, has regulated it by the standard of our self-love, because there is no stronger or more vehement affection."[1]

The words "as thyself" must be read in connection with the previous words, i.e. with the command to love God. When the love of God, the love which flows from God, controls the Christian and he responds and loves God, then self-love will be properly regulated. Love to the neighbor will in reality be love to God, redirected toward the neighbor.

"None can love God, but at the same time he loves himself; for he that loves God, desires to enjoy him; but whosoever desires to enjoy such a good, must needs love himself."[2] The supreme objective of self-love should be self-development toward the image of God. Man was created in the image of God. It was the original purpose of God that man should reflect him. This image or reflection has been ruined by sin. The divine goal has not changed, but can now be reached only through redemption. It is the very purpose of redemption that man might once again reflect the image of God. This is the true condition of our happiness. This aspiration to reflect once again the image of God, this self-love, is a Christian virtue.

---

[1] Jean Calvin, *Institution* (Geneve, Labor et Fides), 1955, Vol. II, Chap. 8, section 54.

[2] William Jenkyn, *An Exposition upon the Epistle of Jude* (London, Samuel Holdsworth), 1839, p. 38a.

Back in 1818, Timothy Dwight commented that "our happiness is a desirable object and deserves to be sought in a certain degree. Our happiness is, in this respect, exactly of the same nature with that of others: it is as truly desirable, and really deserves to be promoted, as that of any created beings whatever . . . the fact, that it is *our* happiness, renders it no more valuable than that of others; so plainly, it does not render it at all less valuable."[3]

To love our neighbor as ourselves might simply mean that we would like to see the image of God recreated and developed in him *as* in ourselves. If it is right to love my neighbor because he is a human being created in the image of God, then it is also right to love myself, since the same holds true for me. There is a self-love which Christians ought to have in accordance with the will of God. We ought to love the divine image in us and in our neighbor. He whose full attention is concentrated on the extension of the kingdom of God, while he neglects to work for the formation of the kingdom of God in his own personality, is not fit to lead others. Such self-love is opposed to egotism and egocentricity.

Divine love is at the root of the service Jesus demands. This is contrary to self-assertion, placing the individual and the particular before the social and the universal, and repudiating the primary law of love. The manifestations of such self-assertion are lust for power and pride. Love is a sacrifical force, but Jesus does not demand the suppression of the true and highest development of the human personality. On the contrary, he aims at the development of man in the image of God, the formation of a balanced, spiritually energetic character. Creativity is encouraged, the personality is set free from momentary impulse and desire, moving under the control of the Spirit of God, who is a Spirit of love. This divine love is the motivating factor of Christian service and leadership.

Service—The Method of Leadership

Jesus came to serve. He was the servant of the Lord par excellence. His service was motivated by love and culminated in death. He served to the point of giving his life. At the same time, he never allowed people to use him for selfish purposes. He never confirmed them in their egotism through his service. His service

[3]Timothy Dwight, *op. cit.*, Vol. III, p. 157 ff.

did not promote the pride of man. The purpose of his service was redemptive, to free man from selfishness and sin as dominating principles.

The Son of man came to serve, said Jesus, and the word he used describes the servant in his activity, rather than in his relationship to his master. The Son of man came to serve, but he spoke with extraordinary authority. He was a stranger to false humility. Service did not degenerate into servility. Greatness is determined by service and humility, not servility and cringing. Jesus humbled himself, but maintained grandeur; he became a servant but retained dignity. He was humble, not subservient.

The service Jesus required goes far beyond the commonly-accepted idea of service. He set the example. In order to teach an unforgettable lesson, he washed the feet of the disciples and reminded them that he was in their midst to serve. His service culminated in self-sacrifice. He gave his life as a ransom, in order to liberate those he served. He used his sovereignty to serve and liberate.

The same attitude is reflected in Paul, who made himself a slave to all in order to save some (I Cor. 9:19). Paul, the leader, freely and happily became a servant. He was at the disposal of others; he was not his own; this is the most legitimate use of Christian freedom. He never negated his rights, but chose to give himself to others. This was at the heart of his methodology.

We cannot allow the idea of service to remain vague. This concept must be illuminated by the life of Christ. He came to serve and demanded that the leaders should serve . . . even as he served. His life culminated in death. The sinful state of mankind left him no alternative but the surrender of his life, to redeem men and set them free.

While the discussion raged among the Twelve regarding greatness, authority, being the first, or leadership, Jesus declared: "The Son of man came not to be served but to serve, and to give his life as a ransom for many." The context is of supreme importance. Greatness is not founded on rank or position, but on service. Greatness is not related to possessions . . . The Son of man had no place to lay his head. Greatness is not determined by power. Despotic rule is powerful, but tyrannical, resulting in bondage.

Christian leadership is redemptive, resulting in freedom, not subjugation. To be great it is necessary to serve, even as Christ served—a service which is redemptive in nature. Jesus makes it clear that Christian leadership is rooted in love, issues in service, aims at redemption, and leads to freedom.

How did Christ serve? His ministry was preeminently one of teaching. Teaching in word and deed consumed the major part of his time. Luke called his first volume a summary of all that Jesus began to do and teach (Acts 1:1), and the Gospel according to Luke covers everything from the infancy to the ascension. Jesus preached his life and lived his doctrine. There was no chasm between doctrine and life, word and talk, revelation and fulfillment. His teaching was redemptive, aimed to set man free.

His actions were didactic; his miracles were redemptive, liberating, healing, and restoring signs.

His teaching was authoritative. Every one of the Gospels records the fact that Jesus spoke with authority. At the conclusion of the Sermon on the Mount the crowds were astonished at his teaching, for he taught them as one who had authority. When he was questioned regarding the source of his authority, he told the parable of the wicked husbandmen (Mk. 12:1-12), wherein he sharply differentiated between the servants sent to obtain the fruit of the vineyard and the son, heir of all things. He did not hesitate to claim divine authority for his words and teaching. He served through his teaching.

Another significant aspect of Christ's ministry was training, especially the training of the Apostles. He spent many hours alone with the Twelve to secure representatives and witnesses and to lay the foundation of the kingdom of God in their lives.

His teaching was unique, inexhaustible, full of declaration, invitation, pleading, promise; it was always holy, spiritual and universally valid. His teaching and training were such that upon reviewing his life he could say: "I have manifested thy name to the men whom thou gavest me . . . they have believed that thou didst send me . . . I kept them . . . I have guarded them . . . I have given them thy word" (John 17).

His service implied obedience but not passivity. For Christ, to serve meant to expend himself on the part of others. Still, he would not allow people to use him for selfish purposes. He refused, for instance, to get involved in settling a legal dispute between two brothers regarding an inheritance (Lk. 12:13 ff). He was not always available, regardless of the nature of the service requested.

A machine *serves* a specific purpose, but without generosity, without nobility, uninspired by love, and unconcerned. Christian service is inspired by love and aims at setting man free.

The service of Jesus was largely carried out through teaching and training in word and deed. He requires the same of Christian leaders today.

Redemption—The Goal of Leadership

The ultimate purpose of Christ was redemptive. The final goal of his life and death, of his teaching and training, of his service and ministry, was to give his life as a ransom, i.e. to deliver from sin, release from captivity, lead to emancipation. Through redemption, man is set free from the controlling power of sin, thus enabled to *serve* God and man. The Christian is set free to serve. The freedom obtained through Jesus Christ is real; it is not an abstract notion, but enables the Christian to submit himself joyfully to the law of love and the sovereignty of God. Freedom is not anarchy, it is not chaotic, it is not without context or framework. Liberated from the controlling principle of sin, freed from momentary impulse, lust and passion, the Christian joyfully places himself under the control of the Holy Spirit and freely responds to the love of God.

God used Moses to redeem and liberate Israel out of Egypt. The aim of Christ was broader—to redeem mankind. He accomplished it through his atoning death. Liberty and service are but opposite sides of the same fact; both are based on redemption.

Only he who lives and moves in agreement with his proper being is really free. He can unfold his personality unhindered and undisturbed. The "proper being" of man is discovered in the original purpose of God, that man should reflect the divine image. But the image was ruined and freedom lost. Personality came under the controlling influence and power of sin. The ability to serve God and man freely was forfeited. Man came under bondage and was enslaved. Only God could liberate man, and he made it possible through redemption. When the objective fact of redemption is subjectively appropriated, man is recreated in the image of God. Once again he is enabled to fulfill God's original purpose: to live a life controlled by the law of love. To be free under grace is the destination of every Christian. The redeemed man, the free man, is under grace, surrendered and glad to serve. He is set free by Christ in order to serve as Christ himself served, by word and deed, teaching and training. True Christian leadership is redemptive, i.e. liberating! The purpose is never to enslave or to subjugate.

This redemptive concept dominates the relationship between the leader and the group. It is a living, dynamic relationship, and the group is not merely seen as a whirling machine. Martin Buber said of Napoleon that he did not know the dimension of the *thou,* that to him all being was *valore,* that he had no one whom he recognized as a being. Some men subject "being" to "having" and establish only business relations with other people. They are not at anyone's disposal, but look upon the whole world as serving their private ends.

The Christian leader, the redemptive leader, will not use the group to achieve selfish purposes with total disregard for the persons who make up the group. After the episode of the golden calf, Moses, the great redemptive leader of Israel, turned to God in prayer on behalf of the nation. God had hinted at the destruction of the nation and promised to make Moses into a great nation, but Moses, against whom they had rebelled, turns to God in intercessory prayer, saying: If thou will forgive their sin—and if not, blot me, I pray thee, out of thy book (Ex. 32:32). Not destruction, but emancipation was his goal. His primary concern was far broader than the narrow focus of his own personality.

The practical applications of this Christian concept of leadership are far reaching. Other theories of leadership may introduce the idea of service and seek adequate motivation. But the redemptive view of the leadership role is distinctly—and essentially—Christian.

7

Leadership Traits

The Christian view of leadership which has just been described does not automatically determine the style of leadership to be adopted, nor does it necessarily rule out any one style. The Christian leader's distinct motivation and aim will influence his methodology, but not press him into a definite mold.

It should not be assumed that such a view of leadership invariably leads to adopting the democratic style. The strengths and weaknesses of this particular approach neither increase nor diminish because of Christian motivation and purpose. The style to be adopted is determined by the single question: How can I best exercise redemptive Christian leadership? This, in turn, is determined by three distinct factors:

The personality of the leader
The expectation of the group
The actual situation

The Personality of the Leader

For centuries it was assumed that leadership was in the nature of an inheritance, that leaders were born, not made. This point of view was combined with the idea that leadership was a monopoly of the aristocracy. With the advent of equalitarian democracy the leadership notion changed. Leadership, it seemed, could be learned; it could be taught as an art, and was open to all.

Innate or acquired, it remains true that the leader brings to the situation certain individual qualities, a certain character structure, a definite profile and capacity. True, possessing the seemingly necessary leadership qualifications does not automatically guarantee success. There also must be a willingness to pay the price, to shoulder the responsibility. The necessary motivation may be lacking, and talent without motivation is inert and of little use.

True, again, it is almost impossible to find a consistent pattern of personality traits characterizing leaders. This could be due to the fact that our measuring instruments do not allow us to determine precisely what the required qualities are so that we can only generalize. Again, it could be that these characteristics are not necessary in equal measure in every leadership situation.

True once more, leadership does not exist in a vacuum. The group and the situation must be considered. Timing is significant, gears have to mesh, the leadership which is provided must be required by the group. All the ingredients have to blend for effective leadership.

Having said all this, it remains true that the personality of the leader plays a key role. The true leader is carried on a tide but he gives the tide unique articulation. "Once the stage is set, the presence of an outstanding leader is indispensable. Without him there will be no movement. The ripeness of the times does not automatically produce a mass movement, nor can elections, laws, and administrative bureaus hatch one . . . it needs the iron will, daring and vision of an exceptional leader to concert and mobilize existing attitudes and impulses into the collective drive of a mass movement. The leader personifies the certitude of the creed and the defiance and grandeur of power."[1]

The leader kindles the vision, evokes enthusiasm, speaks the prophetic word, galvanizes into action, fuses diversity into unity, transforms desire into achievement.

It is difficult to draw up a list of leadership traits. A look at great leaders of the past will reveal striking character differences. The eminent historian Samuel Elliot Morison portrays George Washington as follows: "His superiority lay in character, not talents. He had the power of inspiring respect, but not the gift of popu-

[1]Eric Hoffer, *The True Believer* (N.Y., Harper & Row), 1966, p. 104.

larity. He was direct, not adroit, stubborn rather than flexible; slow to reach a decision rather than a man of quick perception. The mask of dignity and reserve that concealed his inner life came from humility and stern self-control. A warm heart was revealed by innumerable kindly acts to his dependents and subordinates." The same author sees Abraham Lincoln as a man with "innate tact and delicacy that carried conviction of his moral and intellectual greatness to all but the most obtuse, and a humanity that has opened the hearts of all men to him in the end." Elsewhere he writes that Lincoln "emerged humble before God, but the master of men. He seemed to have captured all the greater qualities of the great Americans who preceded him, without their defects; the poise of Washington without his aloofness, the mental audacity of Hamilton without his insolence, the astuteness of Jefferson without his indirection, the conscience of John Quincy Adams without his harshness, the courage of Jackson without his irascibility, the magnetism of Clay without his vanity, the lucidity of Webster without his ponderousness, and fused them with a sincerity and magnanimity that were peculiarly his." Men who occupied the same office brought different leadership qualities to the position. Speaking of President Jackson the same authority avers that he was "ill educated, intolerant, yet professing the immortal principles of the Declaration of Independence."[2]

The heroes and leaders mentioned in Hebrews 11 are as varied in characteristics as the situation required. The same list names Abel, Isaac, Abraham and Joseph, Moses and Gideon, Samson and David. Both Thomas and Peter were part of the apostolic circle, and in church history no greater contrast can be established than between Tertullian and Luther, Calvin and Wesley, or Thomas Aquinas and William Carey. Different ages and circumstances demanded different leadership traits.

Desirable leadership traits permit no logical order, but must be arranged in a somewhat haphazard fashion. However, some thought should be given to: strength of character and decisiveness, courage and enthusiasm, imagination and creativity, intelligence or mental alertness, goal-consciousness, sensitivity, verbal facility and communication. Then there is always the matter of physical health,

---

[2]Samuel Eliot Morison, *op. cit.*, pp. 318, 618, 651.

personal attractiveness, education and experience, achievement, reputation, adaptability and excellence.

Strength of Character

Leadership requires strength of character because of the cost involved, the responsibilities to be shouldered, and the tensions to be endured. Both Moses and Gideon hesitated to assume the burden of leadership. The risk is high. Amos and Jeremiah became extremely unpopular. Luther stood alone before the Diet of Worms, unwilling to "recant one jot or tittle," regardless of pressure. Galileo before the papal court, Socrates in his prison cell, and men of similar temper were unable to yield or compromise and paid a high price for the role of leadership.

It is not easy to persist regardless of the odds. Misfortunes overtook Rembrandt after 1660. His popularity as a painter was on the wane. Agents were turning their attention to a younger generation, but Rembrandt was unwilling to make concessions and pursued his own path undauntedly. He was declared bankrupt in 1656. The failure of contemporary taste to accept the ultimate achievement of his later style was a fate that other great artists have suffered in old age. For Rembrandt, the fulfillment of his art was more important than the applause he might have gained, and his triumph was in his ability to spurn compromise.

These may be extreme examples built on exceptional persons but it remains true that great strength of character is a necessary trait of leadership.

According to Karl von Clausewitz, the famous Prussian general and military writer, the most important qualification for any general is not military knowledge, but a superior mind and strength of character. Hoffer goes as far as to write that "exceptional intelligence, noble character and originality seem neither indispensable nor perhaps desirable. The main requirements seem to be: audacity and a joy in defiance; an iron will; a fanatical conviction that he (the leader) is in possession of the one and only truth . . . the most decisive qualities for the effectiveness of a mass movement leader seem to be audacity, fanatical faith in a holy cause, an awareness of the importance of a close-knit collectivity, and, above all, the ability to evoke fervent devotion in a group of able lieutenants . . . the quality of ideas seems to play a minor role in mass movement leadership. What counts is the arrogant gesture, the complete disregard of the opinion of others, the single-handed defiance of the world."[3]

An editorial in *Time* magazine declares that the supreme quality necessary for the office of the President is "at once most obvious and most elusive: character. To vote wisely for a presidential candidate is basically to judge his strength of character—shorthand for the classic moral virtues of courage, justice, and prudence."[4]

In *The Fountainhead,* Roark, the hero says: "Thousands of years ago, the first man discovered how to make fire. He was probably burned at the stake he had taught his brothers to light. He was considered an evildoer who had dealt with a demon mankind dreaded. But thereafter men had fire to keep them warm, to cook their food, to light their caves. He had left them a gift they had not conceived and he had lifted darkness off the earth. Centuries later, the first man invented the wheel. He was probably torn on the rack he had taught his brothers to build. He was considered a transgressor who ventured into forbidden territory. But thereafter, men could travel past any horizon. He had left them a gift they had not conceived and he had opened the roads of the world. . . .

"Throughout the centuries there were men who took first steps down new roads armed with nothing but their own vision. Their goals differed, but they all had this in common: that the step was first, the road was new, the vision unborrowed, and the response they received—hatred. The great creators—the thinkers, the artists, the scientists, the inventors—stood alone against the men of their time. Every great new thought was opposed. Every great new invention was denounced. The first motor was considered foolish. The airplane was considered impossible. The power loom was considered vicious. Anesthesia was considered sinful. But the men of unborrowed vision went ahead. They fought, they suffered, and they paid. But they won."[5]

Both Eric Hoffer and Ayn Rand put the matter rather forcefully, but we are often told in the New Testament to be strong (I Cor. 16:13; Eph. 6:10; II Tim. 2:1). Bonhoeffer, commenting

[3]Eric Hoffer, *op. cit., pp.* 105–106.
[4]*TIME* Magazine, July 26, 1968.
[5]Ayn Rand, *The Fountainhead* (N.Y., New American Library), 1968, p. 679.

on this thought raises the question: "Is not the weakness of men often more dangerous than deliberate malice? I mean such things as stupidity, lack of independence, forgetfulness, laziness, idleness, corruption, being lead easily astray, etc." Elsewhere he adds that it is the characteristic excellence of the strong man that he can bring momentous issues to the fore and make a decision about them. The weak are always forced to decide between alternatives they have not chosen themselves.[6]

The strength demanded by the Scriptures is not synonymous with independence, self-sufficiency, selfishness, and defiance. The term implies obedience and dedication, loyalty and service. This strength is rooted in God. The Christian is admonished to persevere, to remain steadfast, courageous, transforming obstacles into stepping stones. God gives this steadiness, this ability to bear things, to pass the breaking point without breaking, and to greet the unseen with a cheer.[7] Such strength is needed to make the necessary decisions, for daring and courage, for purposeful action.

Decisiveness

The leader must possess the ability to make decisions without unnecessary delay. Bonhoeffer echoes a word of Christ when he says that "only in doing, can there be submission to the will of God."[8] It is vital to translate thought into action, i.e. to decide. Action springs not from thought alone, but from a readiness for responsibility.

Decisiveness is largely a matter of practice and experience. Some people never stop accumulating evidence and never cease to consider alternate possibilities.

Roger Bellows furnishes a magnificent illustration of indecision: An anecdote is sometimes told of vacillation: a mule stands in the center of a circle; all around its circumference is a ring of fragrant hay. The mule is hungry. There is no wind blowing, no breeze to waft the fragrance more strongly from one direction than another. The goals, equally attractive, surround the mule. He remains in the center and starves to death.

---

[6]Dietrich Bonhoeffer, *Letters and Papers from Prison* (N.Y., Macmillan Co.), 1962, pp. 244 and 233.
[7]Dietrich Bonhoeffer, *Ethics* (N.Y., Macmillan Co.), 1965, p. 43.
[8]Dietrich Bonhoeffer, *op. cit.*, pp. 37, 38.

Men of faith have always been men of action, i.e. men of decision. Occasionally Christian leaders find it extremely difficult to be decisive and to act promptly. Perhaps they dimly feel that action implies self-confidence which might be akin to pride. They remember that God is at work in us, both to will and to work for his good pleasure, but they hesitate (Phil. 2:13).

Christians have received a new governing disposition through the power of the Holy Spirit. This new inclination is the basis for holy volitions and actions. It is in this fashion that God is at work in us. For that matter, and in a broad sense, the devil is at work in the sons of disobedience (Eph. 2:2)—where the same Greek word is used as in Phil. 2:13. Paul does not mean that Satan creates evil volitions in the minds of the non-Christian, not any more than God immediately creates virtuous volitions in the Christian. God creates in us a new heart, a right spirit, a new disposition which becomes the basis of new volition and action. It is in this sense that God is at work in us. The text is not an exhortation to passivity.

Prayer cannot take the place of action flowing from decision. During the rebellion of Absalom, David was told that Ahithophel was on the side of the conspirators. David said: O Lord, I pray thee, turn the counsel of Ahithophel into foolishness. Then David met his trusted adviser and suggested that Hushai join Absalom in order to defeat the counsel of Ahithophel. David prayed that God would destroy the advice of Ahithophel, but he *also* sent Hushai to Absalom to accomplish his aim (II Sam. 15:31-34).

The thought that it is Christ in us working through us, may tend to produce a passivity which is not biblical. Paul, keenly conscious of the fact that he worked more than anyone else, admitted: ". . . it was not I, but the grace of God which is with me" (I Cor. 15:10). He recognized both the efficacy of God's grace and his personal effort. The grace of God is "with me," i.e. in efficient fellowship with me. Paul did not disclaim his active share in bringing about results, but he knew that the divine grace *outweighed* his own activity. To the alternative, whether he or grace had wrought such great things, Paul could only answer as he did: not I, but the grace of God with me. Paul recognized the preponderance of grace, but did not underestimate his personality or activity.

Paralysis results from fear, and fear is expelled by love. "Perfect love casts out fear" (I Jn. 4:18). The confidence that God is for us and with us, the redemptive activity of Christ and his intercession, the illumination and guidance of the Holy Spirit should enable the Christian to act decisively and courageously. The Christian leader lives with quiet resolution, willing to take risks, accepting full responsibility for decisions, with the courage to survive disappointment, not dwelling on success nor accepting discouragement. Faith is always *working* through love, and inactivity or passivity is not an indication of strong faith.

The admonition to prove the will of God (Rom. 12:2), to learn what is pleasing to the Lord (Eph. 5:10) "shows the error of the view that the simple recognition of the will of God must take the form of an intuition which excludes any sort of reflexion and that it must be the naive grasping of the first thought or feeling to force itself upon the mind . . . (The will of God) is something new and different in each different situation in life, and for this reason a man must ever anew examine what the will of God may be."[9]

The Christian, conscious of the will of God, prays with Moses: "If thy presence will not go with me, do not carry us up from here" (Exod. 33:15). But the desire to do the will of God should not produce inertia or indecision. Men of God have never been characterized by passivity.

If the basic purpose is to do the will of God, then the Christian leader can move forward with confidence toward the ultimate goal. Paul had been called to proclaim Christ to the gentiles, but at one time he was forbidden to speak the word in Asia, and the Holy Spirit would not allow him to go into Bithynia (Acts 16:6, 7). We do not know if Paul was restrained from his purpose by inward motivation or prophetic utterance, by vision or by right judgment of circumstances. There was a conflict between human plans and divine direction, but since the basic purpose of Paul was to do the will of God, he was kept from serious error and was, by extraordinary intimation, redirected by the Holy Spirit.

Luke, the historian, relates that Paul was "appointed to go up to Jerusalem" and that he was sent on his way by the church. When the apostle himself relates the incident he says "I went up

---

[9]*Ibid.*

by revelation" (Acts 15:2,3; Gal. 2:2). His subjective analysis differed from the objective viewpoint of the historian. Paul went in compliance with a divine command. It is impossible to determine whether the revelation was first, and the action of the church subsequent, or vice versa.

At another point, Paul explains that he fell into a trance and heard the voice of God telling him to leave Jerusalem immediately (Acts 22:17 ff). The historian informs us that some sought to kill Paul and therefore the believers brought him down to Caesarea and sent him off to Tarsus (Acts 9:29,30 cf. Gal. 1:17). Paul's circumstances (Acts 9), a vision (Acts 22), and a personal decision (Gal. 1) coincided. The essential is to walk in fellowship with God—to walk—which is voluntary, constant, and progressive action.

Jeremiah received an announcement from God that his cousin would offer him a field to buy in Anathoth. The event took place in accordance with the word of God and Jeremiah exclaimed: "Then I knew that this was the word of the Lord" (Jer. 32:6-8). The message was received, the event took place, and the absolute conviction was gained by the prophet that he had correctly heard and understood the word of God. The action, the circumstances and the divine communication all coincided to give the prophet the necessary assurance.

It is taken for granted that the Christian leader is anxious to do the will of God and that commitment to God is his basic motivation. At the same time it would be unreasonable to expect distinct guidance in every single decision, small or large, temporary or permanent. Openness toward God and reliance upon God are characteristic of the Christian leader, without diminishing his decisiveness or impairing his ability to act.

The logical result of absolute certainty regarding the will of God in every phase would lead to infallibility. Is this the reason why Christian leaders find it difficult to admit failure or error? Such a view of divine guidance might easily lead to the most absolute dictatorship under the guise of Christian commitment.

On the other hand it is equally wrong to rationalize indecisiveness by referring to prayer and by claiming insufficient knowledge regarding the will of God. This would be embracing the other horn of the dilemma.

"God treats the leader as a mature adult, leaving more and more to his spiritual discernment, and giving fewer sensible and tangible evidences of his guidance than in earlier years. This perplexity adds to the inevitable pressures incidental to any responsible office."[10] Constant and absolute certainty regarding the will of God would exclude the elements of daring and risk which are vital components of the Christian faith. It is the mark of spiritless man to venture only where the probabilities are favorable.

Great Christian leaders have been characterized by a willingness to commit themselves with enthusiasm in the face of the seemingly impossible, and to identify themselves with causes that needed to be served rather than with those guaranteeing success. The inept and unfit will seldom innovate. The successful will rarely advocate drastic change. Only the courageous and creative leader will take the necessary initiative to pioneer and to venture. In this sense true leadership and security are basically incompatible.

To develop decisiveness:

1. Recognize the problem, specify information.
2. Get the facts—not opinions.
3. Classify—distinguish essential and nonessential.
4. Develop a trial solution.
5. Seek cooperation (including consultation).
6. Don't try to anticipate everything.
7. Adopt a decision.
8. Move into action.
9. Don't be afraid of making a wrong decision.

Once a decision is made, move on to something else. Post-decision steadfastness is as important as pre-decision certitude.

There are four key questions in decision making:

1. Do I really understand the problem?
   What is the cause?
2. What am I trying to accomplish?
   What is the purpose?

---

[10]J. Oswald Sanders, *Spiritual Leadership* (Chicago, Ill., Moody Press) 1967, p. 112.

3. Is this the best way?
   What are the alternatives?
4. If I do it this way, what can go wrong?
   What are the consequences?

Some of these attitudes are illustrated in the life of Philip. He analyzed the problem when he estimated that it would take 200 denarii to buy enough bread for the hungry crowd. The lad with five loaves and two fish did not represent a genuine solution. Personal resources and group resources were inadequate. It took a great deal of courage to organize the crowd in groups of 50 and 100 and to expect decisive action from Jesus.

At times decisions have to be taken immediately. Delays cannot be tolerated. The Cuban missile crisis is a case in point. Robert F. Kennedy favored a blockade of Cuba not from a deep conviction that it would be a successful course of action, but from a feeling that it had more flexibility and fewer liabilities than a military attack. At times, decisions have to be based on incomplete data. If so, the most flexible solution should probably be adopted to allow for necessary changes.

Courage

A leader needs courage because leadership involves risk. Courage is necessary to overcome the anguish, the loneliness, perhaps the ridicule and the rejection. The possibility of failure often looms large.

The derivation of the word "courage" indicates its relation to the heart, the center and focus of life. Courage comes from the French word *coeur,* i.e. heart. Courage means "that a man is not divided, or in doubt; he does not stand in his own way, he is not consumed by self-contradiction, nor does he deceive himself. He affirms himself, and does not give up. It is different with the man whose heart fails him, who capitulates before difficulties, who is discouraged by them and is therefore his own betrayer, and gives up."[11]

---

[11]Gerhard Ebeling, *The Nature of Faith* (Wm. Collins Sons & Co.), 1961, p. 102.

In his last letter addressed to a leader of the church, Paul reminds Timothy to rekindle the gift of God which is in him "for God did not give us a spirit of timidity but a spirit of power and love and self-control" (II Tim. 1:7). Positively expressed, God gives us courage, heart—and this must be preeminently so in the case of a leader. Thomas is an outstanding example. Loyal to the person of Christ, but despairing of the cause, he was willing to die with his Master (John 11:16).

The redemptive leader must have a courage which might be called "the courage of the invisible," i.e. the courage to reject an immediate ephemeral success in the interest of the ultimate goal. It takes a great deal of courage to endure the reproach of being unsuccessful. In the words of Ogden Nash:

> I hardly suppose I know anybody who wouldn't
> rather be a success than a failure,
> Just as I suppose every piece of crabgrass in
> the garden would much rather be an azalea.

At times it is not easy to evaluate success and failure. Often it appeared that Paul had setback upon setback. Nevertheless, he finally reached Rome which had been one of his long-range goals. Success has been described as a progressive realization of goals, and in this light Paul was eminently successful.

Success in life depends on amplitude of possibilities. Every blow we receive must serve as another impulse towards new attempts. "The key word here is *incitement*. In physics, one thing does not incite another; it causes it and the cause produces an effect in proportion to itself. A billiard ball colliding with another imparts to it an impulse in principle equal to its own; cause and effect are equal. But when the spur's point ever so lightly touches its flank, the thoroughbred breaks into a gallop, generously out of proportion to the impulse of the spur. The reaction of the horse, rather than a response to an outer impulse, is a release of exuberant inner energies."[12] It is this elasticity and vigor, such creative power, which is necessary for success.

---

[12]Ortega y Gasset, *History as a System* (N.Y., W. W. Norton & Co.), 1962, p. 20.

As long as a leader is successful, he is regarded by others as equipped with the authority of heaven. In case of failure, the same people are swift to detect a rift between him and God. All too often, God is identified with success. The passion for success here and now is characteristic of an age impatient with long-range objectives, distant goals, slow developments and spiritual concerns.

Christ faced outraged prejudice, wounded pride and threatened privilege. He persevered in his vocation, fully aware of the fact that every step he took made the end more certain. Conscious of danger he proceeded in the face of it with calm and firmness. He acted courageously in a threatening situation. Courage to speak boldly, to act vigorously, to proceed regardless of criticism, without ever losing sight of the goal—such courage is vital to leadership. Men of faith have conquered kingdoms, enforced justice and refused to accept release in spite of torture. In many ways the Judges of Israel were a strange group of leaders, but they had the courage to act, and this was what the moment demanded. After the death of Moses and when the word of God came to Joshua, the new leader of Israel, the essence of the divine message was: Only be strong and very courageous!

The leader needs the courage to say with William B. Travis, surrounded at San Antonio by vastly superior forces: I shall never surrender or retreat . . . Victory or death.

At a crucial moment of his career, Pizarro, drawing his sword, traced a line with it on the sand from east to west and, turning towards the south, said: "Friends and comrades, on that side are toil, hunger, nakedness, the drenching storm, desertion and death; on this side ease and pleasure. There lies Peru with its riches; here Panama and its poverty. Choose, each man, what best becomes a brave Castillian. For my part, I go to the south." Pizarro stepped across the line and thirteen men followed.[13] This small band, with death rather than riches as a reward, chose honor and stood firm with their leader. A handful of men, without food, without clothing, almost without arms, without knowledge of the land to which they were bound, without vessel to transport them, were left on a lonely rock in the ocean with the avowed purpose

[13]William H. Prescott, *The Conquest of Peru* (N.Y., New American Library), 1961, p. 169.

of carrying a crusade against a powerful empire, staking their lives on its success. Gold was the driving motivation! The higher motivation of Christian leadership should inspire no less courage and determination. The demand for courage is all the more severe for a Christian leader because it is the courage of the invisible.

Enthusiasm

Christian courage is sustained by courage and hope. "It might be said that, in a sense, hope is not interested in the *how*: and this fact shows how fundamentally untechnical it is, for technical thought, by definition, never separates the consideration of ends and means. An end does not exist for the technician, if he does not see approximately how to achieve it. This however, is not true for the inventor or the discoverer who says, 'There must be a way' and who adds: 'I am going to find it.' He who hopes says simply: 'It will be found.' "[14] Serve the Lord enthusiastically; never flag in zeal, never be lazy. Be earnest, eager (Rom. 12:11). The Greek word denotes the moral earnestness Christians should apply to their vocation.

The word "enthusiasm" is derived from the Greek *en + theos* literally "in God," i.e. inspired by God, animated by God, a divinely inspired interest or zeal. Enthusiasm is an intense, exalted emotion; it is a source of zeal and purposeful action (John. 2:17). Enthusiasm looks into the future and commits itself in the face of the seemingly impossible. To the Christian enthusiast, the probabilities are always favorable. He is conscious of the fact that God is with him. The enthusiastic Christian leader echoes the triumphant words of Paul: "In all these things we are more than conquerors through him who loved us. For I am sure that neither death, nor life, nor angels, nor principalities, nor things present, nor things to come, now powers, nor height, nor depth, nor anything else in all creation, will be able to separate us from the love of God in Christ Jesus our Lord" (Rom. 8:37-38). This assurance is based on the fact that "God is for us" (v.31). This conviction sustains enthusiasm. It is one of the true marks of leadership.

Fortunately, every leader need not be a genius, but each one must have surgency, a quality which is defined in terms of cheer-

[14]Gabriel Marcel, *Homo Viator* (N.Y., Harper & Row), 1962, pp. 51–52.

fulness, geniality, expressiveness, alertness, originality and enthusiasm. Enthusiasm is really a cheerful, optimistic, positive attitude. It is contagious and demonstrates that the leader understands and believes in his own mission. Such a note of fervency and intenseness is characteristic of men of faith. Theirs is a moral and spiritual vitality, a keen and ardent interest. This does not keep them from sound emotional balance. Indeed, the leader must be a well-adjusted person because the erratic, inconsistent, and ambivalent man will create disharmonies and uncertainties.

"How should we then go to meet the future? When the sailor is out upon the sea, when everything is changing about him, when the waves are constantly born and die, then he does not stare down into the depths of these, for they change. He looks up at the stars: and why? Because they are faithful; as they stand now, they stood for the patriarchs, and will stand for the coming generations. By what means does he then conquer the changing conditions? Through the eternal. Through the eternal can one conquer the future, because the eternal is the foundation of the future; therefore through this one can understand that. What then is the eternal power in man? It is faith. What is the expectation of faith? Victory, or as the Scriptures have so earnestly and so movingly taught us, it is that all things must work together for good to those that love God."[15]

As Kierkegaard put it elsewhere: Not until a man is finished with the future can he be entirely and undividedly in the present. It is only by conquering the future that he is finished with the future, and this is exactly the work of faith, for its expectation is victory.

To sustain enthusiasm regardless of the circumstances, to hope against hope, to maintain zeal in spite of reverses, such a quality is truly born of God.

"When passion is simply a frenzy of turbulent emotion, it is of no use at all. Anyone can be passionate, that way. But it is not so easy to maintain that sort of fire which is both critical and creative, that incandescence so supplied with thermal energy that it will not be cooled when the two coldest things in the world come to lodge within it: cool logic and an iron will. The vulgar, false,

---

[15]Soren Kierkegaard, *Edifying Discourses* (Collins, 1958), pp. 33–34.

impotent sort of passion shrinks in terror from the proximity of reflective thought, for it senses that at such a chilly contact it will be frozen out of existence. Hence the symptom of high creative passion is that it seeks to complete itself by uniting with the cooler virtues; that it admits of reflective criticism, without losing its creative energy. It is fire supported with the constancy of clear understanding and a calm will."[16]

Genuine enthusiasm is not merely youthful energy and a burning desire to change the whole world. It is more than the first burst of joy or youthful ambition to fight. It is difficult to maintain enthusiasm in the face of "a small and despised task that is to be done; when one does not defy a world which cheated one's expectation, but sits there abandoned by the great expectation concerning oneself, deprived of every evasion; when no broad prospect tempts one to dare the venture, but one sits inactive, despondent before the humble task of patience, which becomes even more humble because time is wasted in dreaming youth's dreams over again." Or again, enthusiasm must be sustained "when it is no longer the task to spring forward like a lion, but to remain in the same place and, in spite of all exertion, not be able to move; when the task is not to traverse the world in easy flight, but to endure in a dead calm in which the enthusiasm threatens to expire; when the task is to feel the weakness, and yet not let go the enthusiasm, to hope against hope; when it is the task to endure in the long toilsome drudgery which is inseparable from every enthusiastic enterprise . . . when it is of no avail to rush forward in wild abandon, but it is required that one assume a strait-jacket, and be enthusiastic in it; aye, there is the opportunity to show that one is really enthusiastic."[17]

The negative approach to life always concludes in advance that something cannot be done, without even trying and in the absence of contrary evidence. This is not rational. In some way we should be more like the man who, when asked if he could play the piano answered: I don't know . . . I have never tried.

Enthusiasm must be harnessed and channeled constructively.

---

[16]Ortega y Gasset, *Mission of the University* (N.Y., W. W. Norton & Co.), 1966, pp. 18–19.
[17]Soren Kierkegaard, *op. cit.*, pp. 182–183.

Francis of Assisi was neither an organizer nor an administrator. He was too impulsive, too unpredictable to carry the load of a great organization. The actual management of the order soon passed into the hands of others. The dynamic, charismatic personality of Francis painted a primitive ideal which seemed unattainable. His ardent devotion and enthusiastic missionary endeavor, the poetic strain of his soul were beyond limitation. Unfortunately, his lack of organizational ability created rivalries and factions. The history of the order was explosive. The moderates wished to maintain something of the primitive poverty but at the same time establish themselves in universities and develop scholars. The zealots, or spirituals, hoped to maintain the monastic order in its purity. At the other extreme there were those who desired a complete relaxation of the rule of poverty. In spite of deep devotion and flaming enthusiasm, Francis failed as an organizer because he did not achieve the necessary balance.

Creativity

Creativity is linked with imagination. The ability to imagine is the ability to create in advance, in one's own mind, a new plan, a new line of action. Creative imagination is the ability to conceive of that which is merely seen in fragments or on the surface as a complete, perfected, integral whole. It is not fantasy nor fantastic, but constructive and creative. Wordsworth speaks of

> Imagination, which, in truth
> Is but another name for absolute power
> And clearest insight, amplitude of mind,
> And Reason in her most exalted mood.

When God pours out his spirit upon all flesh "young men shall see visions, and old men shall dream dreams" (Acts 2:17).

David Sarnoff of RCA once explained that because of his limited knowledge, as compared to the technical experts, he was not troubled by the difficulties which they could see. Therefore he placed no brakes on his imagination and presented his dreams with conviction. Most of them were ultimately realized. Sarnoff found that it was wonderful to have an imagination unrestrained by the slightest knowledge of the facts. He concluded that the more he lived in the world of science and technology, the more he became convinced that the practical men in this field are the dreamers.

Without imagination there can be no creative activity. Creative leaders must have this extraordinary sensitivity to their surroundings and the ability to see things to which the average person is blind. To combine the images of past sensations into fresh groups for purposes of our own, to use these images to symbolize abstract ideas, this is the power of imagination at work. The skill to go beyond the obvious limitations of a problem, the capacity to discover new dimensions to the problem, the willingness to deviate from established norms—these are some of the characteristics of the creative person.

Creativeness means in the first instance imagining something different, better, and higher. Imagination calls up before us something better than the reality around us. Creativeness always rises above reality. Creativity should not be confused with productivity. The latter is simply "more of the same," but creativity is innovation, transcending the established order of things.

To the Christian leader creativeness is a work of man's God-like freedom, the revelation of the image of the Creator within him. In the redeemed man this image has been recreated and is brighter, and consciously reflected. The creative imagination has been renewed. Creativeness is activity together with God. The creative act is a daring upsurge, moving beyond normal limitations and conditions.

According to Berdyaev, creativity is inseparable from freedom. "Only he who is free creates. Out of necessity can be born only evolution; creativity is born of liberty."[18] This freedom must be defined. It is neither negative, nor arbitrary, nor without content nor void. Such freedom would lead to emptiness and non-being. Rather, it is Christian freedom, freedom under God, freedom of which the content is love. Such freedom is the desirable atmosphere for creativity. Such freedom issues in service, whereas lust and passion wants everything for itself, is greedy, insatiable and vam-

---

[18]Nicolas Berdyaev, *The Destiny of Man* (N.Y., Harper & Row), 1960, pp. 142, 137.

pirish. Liberation cannot result in inner emptiness—it is not merely liberation *from* something but also liberation *for the sake of* something. And this "for the sake of" is creativeness. Creativeness is an ascent and presupposes height. Creativeness does not move along a flat surface in endless time, but ascends toward eternity. Where the Spirit of God is there is liberty, and this makes possible the creativeness which is at the service of man.

Liberty and law, freedom and necessity are not mutually exclusive. "Suppose we are in a room with four doors and four windows, the room being on the twentieth floor of a skyscraper. We can make an exit by any four doors. We can dive through one of the windows, but that is not recommended. But we cannot walk through the wall, or instantly sink through the floor, or fly through the ceiling. Ceiling, walls and floor are destiny; the choice of doors is freedom. If there were no destiny in that room, there would be no choice of doors; indeed there would be no room. So freedom without destiny is a vacuum, and destiny without freedom is a steel block."[19] The freedom necessary for creativity does not presuppose organizational anarchy or chaos. The innovator works within a framework, moves toward a goal.

"In studies of creative people one finds many references to a quality that might be described as 'openness.' At one level, openness refers to the individual's receptivity to the sights, sounds, events and ideas that impinge on him. Most of us are skillful in shutting out the world, and what we do observe we see with a jaded eye. Men or women with the gift of originality manage to keep a freshness of perception, an unspoiled awareness. Of course, this openness to experience is limited to those features of the external world that seem to the individual to be relevant to his inner life. No one could be indiscriminately open to all the clutter and clatter of life. The creative individual achieves his heightened awareness of some aspects of life by ignoring other aspects. And since the aspects he ignores are often precisely those routine matters on which the rest of us lavish loving attention, he is often put down as odd."

Gardner adds, "One of the interesting findings contained in

[19]George A. Buttrick, *Christ and History* (N.Y., Abingdon Press), 1963, p. 89.

recent research is that the creative individual as a rule chooses to conform in the routine, everyday matters of life, such as speech, dress, and manners. One gets the impression that he simply is not prepared to waste his energy in nonconformity about trifles. He reserves his independence for what really concerns him—the area in which his creative activities occur. This distinguishes him sharply from the exhibitionists who reject convention in those matters that will gain them the most attention."[20]

That the creative person is often considered odd is well illustrated in the case of Frank Whittle. When he "first presented his idea for a jet engine, he was met with massive indifference from the scientific bureaucracy; they were interested in new problems, but the kind of new problems they were interested in were better pistons, improved propellers, and the like. For the very reason that his idea was brilliant, it failed to mesh with the ideas of the fund-givers of the time, and it got support only because a few men, like Launcelot Law Whyte, decided to back the man."[21]

The observation that creativity is linked to a certain degree of openness deserves special emphasis. The Bible speaks of a certain simplicity or openness which should characterize the Christian. God imparts understanding to the *simple,* the unsophisticated person (Ps. 119:130 cf. 19:7). The Hebrew word translated *simple* is derived from a root meaning *openness,* spreading out. This quality can degenerate into credulity and many warnings are addressed to the *simple* in the book of Proverbs. Balance is desirable. To be simple-minded and guileless can be a serious defect (Rom. 16:18), yet at the same time we are admonished to be simple, guileless (Rom. 16:19). In the latter case the Greek word describes something which is still in its original state, intact, morally innocent. A certain naiveté, artlessness, or ingenuousness is a desirable quality. Such receptivity or openness is related to imagination and creativity.

Creativeness always imagines something better than the existing reality. It is stimulated by dissatisfaction with the status quo, transmuting it into creativity. Discontent is at the root of the creative

[20]John W. Gardner, *op. cit.,* p. 35 ff.
[21]William H. White, Jr., *The Organization Man* (Garden City, N.Y., Doubleday & Co.), 1957, p. 245.

process. Frustration may become a significant factor to lead men to the summit of their creative best. Creativity will be bold, original, distinctive, but should not be turned loose without limit or direction. If it is to be redemptive it must aim at clearly defined goals. "There is no unequivocal evidence that the intellectual is at his creative best when left wholly on his own."[22] Creativity must operate within a definite framework. It is precisely when infused with the desire to furnish redemptive service—which is the true concept of Christian leadership—that creativity can be at its best.

Intellectual ability is an indispensable leadership quality and one related to creativity. As Pascal pointed out: The greater intellect one has, the more originality one finds in men. Ordinary persons find no difference between men.

Dissatisfaction, restlessness, desire for excellence, aspiration to the height, surgency, special drive—these elements are difficult to define and yet absolutely necessary for creativity. To use the same building blocks but to construct something novel, this is creativity. "Let no one say that I have said nothing new; the arrangement of the subject is new. When we play tennis, we both play with the same ball, but one of us places it better.

"I had it as soon said that I used words employed before . . . if the same thoughts in a different arrangement do not form a different discourse, no more do the same words in their different arrangement form different thoughts!"[23]

Creative ideas may come automatically or spontaneously, but not without preliminary conscious thought. There must be intense interest in solving a specific problem or in obtaining a particular answer. This demands data collection, followed by a sifting process of "unconscious separation." Later, in a moment of leisure or mild activity, the idea will come to the forefront. The significance of leisure will be considered later.

Creativity may be a matter of definition. It is a disposition to make valuable innovations. It has been defined as the ability to relate to to connect, sometimes in odd and yet in striking fashion, regardless of the field or discipline. The emphasis falls on novelty because it is the unquestioning acceptance of existing patterns that

[22]Eric Hoffer, *The Ordeal of Change* (N.Y., Harper & Row), 1963, p. 31.
[23]Blaise Pascal, Pensées (N.Y., E. P. Dutton & Co.), 1948, p. 7.

keep people from creativity. The creative act results in something new, original, different. Creativity grasps two realities and draws a spark from juxtaposition.

The process of creativity has been described in the following steps: 1) Desire: there must be a reason to want to create something original. It may be the expression of a personal experience or the solution of a problem or the response to a changing environment. At any rate, creativity starts with motivation. 2) Preparation: the first step towards satisfying desire is to gather pertinent information. This can be done through research, experimentation, analysis, and all other gathering of data. 3) Synthesis: There is an effort to discover a new pattern, to attempt new relationships, to bring together hitherto unrelated concepts. 4) Incubation: generally speaking, the solution does not appear immediately. The problem is "dropped" but the unconscious mind keeps struggling with the problem. 5) Intimation: the feeling develops that a solution is at hand. Something wells up into the conscious mind "like the light before the dawn." This is naturally followed by 6) Illumination: the word is Eureka! Insight is gained. Everything appears with clarity. 7) Verification: the new concept is examined and evaluated. Perhaps a theory can be tested, the work of art exhibited, the invention tried. The creative process has been completed.

Intelligence

The "leading men among the brethren" (Acts 15:22), were "those of the first rank," men whose judgment was deliberate and careful, based on due considerations after weighing and comparing the facts. This is the full meaning of the word translated "leading."

Intelligence is indispensable. Intelligence has been defined as the capacity to profit by experience or as the ability to solve problems. The leader must be intelligent; he must have the ability to use knowledge purposefully. Reason has been defined as man's ability to receive, to process and to communicate information. Thinking requires a state of focused awareness. The leader must possess mental alertness, the ability to deal competently with situations as they arise. This mental power, this cognitive capacity, this ability to understand, this aptitude to grasp truth and to discover meaning is indispensable for true Christian leadership.

It is a popular misconception to assume that great talent is highly specific. We assume that the man of high talent is narrowly gifted. We imagine that the great painters, musicians, political leaders, or inventors could function in only one specific area. Research evidence indicates that gifted persons have many talents and that they could use their intelligence, creativity, and all the other component parts of their personality to excel in many different fields. It is true that the superior intelligence of the reasoning man can go wrong. The practical man may be conscious of conditions which the reasoner overlooks. A renewed and wholesome emphasis on common sense may be desirable. "Common sense is what one likes to resort to in difficult situations, to find the natural and simple way against the fantastic and complex. It is a grasp of things as they are and of what must be done. It protects us from general principles which, though correct, are destructive in application, being abstract and blind to reality. Common sense finds what cannot be logically deduced or adequately justified, but will convincingly solve our problems here and now."[24]

In the days of king David 200 key men from the tribe of Issachar joined the king, men who had "understanding of the times, to know what Israel ought to do" (I Chron. 12:32). David himself served the counsel of God in his own generation, because he clearly perceived the needs of his contemporaries (Acts 13:36).

Reason and faith are not seen as antagonists in Scripture. Faith may move beyond reason and transcend reason, but no premium is placed on ignorance nor is reward promised to the unwise. The heroes of faith such as Abraham or Moses were hardly unintelligent.

Revelation does not take the place of reason. Gideon was assured of the will of God. The fleece of wool had been a distinct and unusual sign. In addition, Gideon overheard a dream and its interpretation, giving him further assurance. Direct and indirect revelation combined to give Gideon confidence regarding the outcome of the battle. The army was diminished to 300 in accordance with divine instruction. It seemed a strange strategy. In spite of such extensive and detailed guidance—perhaps seldom experienced today—Gideon employed shrewd tactics. He divided the small elite corps of 300 into three companies, surrounded the camp of the

[24]Karl Jaspers, *op. cit.*, p. 247

enemy, and used a ruse to defeat him (Judg. 6 and 7). The revelation of God's will apprehended by faith did not set aside the intelligent use of reason. Men God used in the history of the church have often been those of remarkable intellect. In the early days, Tertullian, Origen, Clement of Alexandria, and Augustine were men of brilliant intellectual achievement. Illustrations could be multiplied across the pages of history.

The reasoning power of Paul, the wisdom of Stephen, the eloquence of Apollos—the intellectual ability of these and other early leaders of the church and their spiritual dedication laid the foundation for the subsequent spiritual conquest of the Roman Empire.

Intelligence is an indispensable leadership trait. A leader needs the ability to use his mind successfully, to understand, to solve problems and deal competently with situations as they arise. Yes, intelligence is absolutely essential to any form of leadership.

Goal-Consciousness

"A man of understanding sets his face toward wisdom, but the eyes of a fool are on the ends of the earth" (Prov. 17:24). The leader has his eye on the goal, but the fool is aimless. The wise man "sets his face toward wisdom," i.e. wisdom is always before him; it is his aim, his purpose. The eyes of the fool wander aimlessly, distracted, without fixed object, moving to that which is far off. The fool is everywhere with his thoughts except where he ought to be. Ignoring that which lies nearest, he loses himself in that which is remote. He does not have the ability to focus, and flutters about fantastically. That which is of least importance impresses him most.

To live is to be directed toward something, to progress towards a goal. In this sense many people never seem to live but merely to exist. Not that anyone really lives without goals, but some focus on the goal whereas others seem to live unconsciously. In reality, there is always a dominant image toward which we move. The Christian leader helps the group define healthy goals and to focus on these objectives. The greatest satisfaction may not be found in achievement, but in achieving, in growth and development, in movement, in progress toward the goal. Dostoyevsky, in describing the life of convicts in *The House of the Dead,* reflects that "without some goal and some effort to reach it, no man can live."[25]

In the same vein, Ayn Rand comments, "The man whose life lacks direction or purpose, the man who has no creative goal, necessarily feels helpless and out of control; the man who feels helpless and out of control, feels inadequate too and unfit for existence; and the man who feels unfit for existence is incapable of enjoying it."[26]

Goal-consciousness characterizes every true leader. Jesus was no exception. He pursued specific goals. Luke introduces the last journey from Galilee to Jerusalem with these words: "When the days drew near for him to be received up, he set his face to go to Jerusalem" (Lk. 9:51). The time of departure had come. The days were fulfilled and Jesus "steadfastly set his face," literally an expression denoting fixedness of purpose regardless of difficulty or danger.

Jesus had a profound sense of mission. The two Greek verbs translated "to send" are applied fifty-three times to Jesus in the Gospels. He was always conscious of purpose and moved toward a goal. Leaders usually hold steadfastly to a few main principles.

Fellowship is not merely being together but doing things together. It is not primarily a cause which makes men loyal to each other, but the loyalty of men to each other which makes a cause. Men do not achieve great solidarity or preserve it simply by being together. Mutual bonds are forged only by doing things together. The absence of a common purpose is a major source of unhappiness in any group. Both the leader and the group derive satisfaction from activity geared toward specific purposes. A sense of achievement, which is highly important, cannot exist unless there is a clear-cut goal to be attained. This goal-consciousness strengthens morale. Morale has been described as an attitude when hands and feet keep working although the head says it can't be done.

Every leader has a marked degree of purpose. Single motivation gives coherence to the leadership effort. Such singlemindedness creates stability. It is the double-minded, the doubter, who is like a wave of the sea driven and tossed by the wind. The Christian

---

[25]Fyodor Dostoyevsky, *The House of the Dead* (N.Y., Dell Pub. Co.), 1964, p. 302.

[26]Ayn Rand, *The Virtue of Selfishness* (N.Y., New American Library), 1964, p. 62.

leader does not have a "double heart" (Ps. 12:2), literally "a heart and a heart." He has prayed with the Psalmist: unite my heart.

Because the redemptive leader is not an opportunist, his motto is principle rather than expediency. Such a leader does not live with affection beaming in one eye and calculation shining out of the other. He is single-minded, keeping one end in view and making all things serve this one purpose. His life flows from one source and moves toward one goal. In the language of Jesus, his eye is sound, single, looking at one object only, in one direction, focused on one goal. The Christian leader, more than any other, will not attempt to serve two masters. It is in this sense that Solomon admonishes us: Let your eyes look directly forward, and your gaze be straight before you (Prov. 4:25).

In the truest sense, only a Christian leader can have such concentration, such singleness of purpose. He is delivered from the controlling principle of selfishness which is a set of tumultuous and conflicting passions. He has only one desire, whose one desire is God. All else flows from this unique relationship. The Christian leader is willing to serve, teach, train, and exercise a redemptive ministry because he has a single goal in mind. The way of wisdom is the only way which has no bifurcations. Paul expressed his concentration in the words: "One thing I do." Contrast the ideal Christian leader with Napoleon. By his own confession his ultimate objectives were not often clear. In the final analysis it was his own destiny that mattered—and he identified or confused his destiny with the destiny of civilization. As Madame de Stael observed, "He wanted to put his gigantic self in the place of mankind." This is *not* redemptive leadership.

Long-range goals stimulate and galvanize creativity. Creativity moves toward concrete objectives. Such singleness of purpose does not necessarily imply immediate and detailed planning producing rigidity or fixity, detrimental to creativity. Preparatory thinking is not prophetic thinking, but planning remains an essential ingrediant of goal-oriented leadership.

"The significance of anticipatory thinking lies in the illumination of possibilities, not in prediction, and much less in knowledge of the future. We must guard against taking anticipatory thoughts for certainties. If simple, perceptible basic lines for the future seem obvious, if there are decisive guideposts for our planning, the responsible human being is still free to perceive new facts that can make everything look different. But the more open the mind that has perceived the facts, the more it has weighed them, the more profoundly will it approach the last, incalculable choice. Then it will be as impossible to cut the knot blindly, with unscrupulous brutality, as to give up the decision and to lapse into helpless inaction."[27]

Purpose is related to planning. The great centers of civilization have emerged in geographic areas where man was compelled to plan. The yearly inundations of the Nile, the Euphrates, the Ganges, and the Yellow River threatened havoc. Canalization would produce fertility and such a challenge compelled goal-oriented planning. Gradually, these great rivers have been controlled by the organized labor of the masses. States have been founded and governments developed on such planning. The four rivers became four centers of world civilization: Egypt, Babylon, India, and China.

Organization is conscious planning. Because Themistocles had the foresight to advise the Athenians to use all the income from the mines to build a fleet on a par with the Persian fleet, Greece was ultimately saved from military disaster. Ten years later, when Persia attacked, the Athenians were victorious at Salamis. This type of anticipatory thinking and goal-orientation is a key to success.

"When we are really going to do something and have dedicated ourselves to a purpose, we cannot be expected to be ready at hand to look after every passer-by and to lend ourselves to every chance display of altruism. One of the things that most delight travellers in Spain is that if they ask someone in the street where such a building or square is, the man asked will often turn aside from his own path and generously sacrifice himself to the stranger, conducting him to the point he is interested in. I am not going to deny that there may be in this disposition of the worthy Spaniard some element of generosity, and I rejoice that the foreigner so interprets his conduct. But I have never, when hearing or reading of this,

[27]Karl Jaspers, *op. cit.*, p. 283.

been able to repress a suspicion: 'Was my countryman, when thus questioned, really going anywhere?' Because it might well be, in many cases, that the Spaniard is going nowhere, has no purpose or mission, but rather goes out into life to see if others' lives can fill his own a little."[28]

In connection with long-range planning the following questions should be raised:

What is the purpose or the mission?
What are the resources and/or limitations?
Where are the sensitive areas in the world where our ministry might have maximum effectiveness?
What are the criteria for the best choice?
What needs to be done in the next twelve months to implement decisions?

The last question determines priorities and leads to a cost analysis.

Long-range planning is broad strategy; daily implementation is tactics. Strategy deals with wide spaces, large perspectives, and great movement of forces. Tactics is the art and science of fighting battles, the execution of movement for attack or defense. Strategy gives tactics its mission. The goal-consciousness which should characterize the leader is strategy—not tactics.

According to the French, nothing succeeds like success. As mentioned before, success has been defined as the progressive realization of goals. To achieve success there must be orientation toward a goal and progress in that direction. Success per se has little value. But when success is evident in the pursuit of redemptive goals it can only be a cause of rejoicing.

Sensitivity

At one point Paul prayed that the love of the Philippians might grow in discernment or insight (Phil. 1:9), literally "in all perception." Love imparts a sensitive touch, giving a keen edge to the discriminating faculty, in things moral and spiritual. The word Paul uses is concerned with practical applications. "There is no

---

[28]Ortega y Gasset, *The Revolt of the Masses* (N.Y., W. W. Norton & Co.), 1957, p. 143.

rift between the enkindled heart and the enlightened mind. Light without love can be as forbiddingly cold as an iceberg in moonlight. Love without light, on the other hand, can be as flamingly destructive as a forest fire in the dry season."[29] Love as an unregulated impulse is dangerous. Love giving itself to hard thinking and sensitive discrimination is a delight to God and a priceless blessing to the church.

Love brings rare insight. To an eminent degree, perception, discrimination, and even tact are needed by the Christian leader. Tact is the ability to deal with others without creating offense, the talent to say and to do the proper thing at the right time, to make correct moral decisions. Tact involves understanding of human nature and consideration for the feelings of others. In this respect the Christian leader has a distinct advantage, since he lives in the light of God and has gained self-knowledge through his relationship with God. The Bible deals at length with the problem of human nature and sheds light on the topic. Informed by love, tact becomes more natural. Love generates this alertness, this wonderful sensitivity. "The word suggests the nervous organism of the body, all the avenues of approach by the senses of the mind, that wonderful sensitive plate, more delicate than any seismograph for recording earthquake shocks, or any chemical apparatus for detecting affinities between atoms or any electrical machinery for noting the behavior of electrons, while telegraphy requires apparatus for sending and receiving the sound waves. We give various names to this ethical sensitiveness, like tact, spiritual sensibility, a trained conscience."[30]

If tact is a sense of proportion, humor is a sense of disproportion. A light touch, a delicate sense of the incongruous can relieve the strain and tension at a crucial moment. Sidney Smith, speaking of a leader, said: "The meaning of an extraordinary man is that he is eight men in one man; that he has as much wit as if he had no sense, as much sense as if he had no wit; that his conduct is as judicious as if he were the dullest of human beings and his imagination as brilliant as if he were irretrievably ruined."

---

[29]Paul S. Rees, *The Adequate Man* (Westwood, N.J., Fleming H. Revell), 1959, in loco.
[30]A.T. Robertson, *Paul's Joy in Christ.* (Nashville, Tenn., Broadman Press), 1959, in loco.

Persuasiveness

Christian leadership involves redemptive service which in turn implies teaching. This underscores the importance of communication and persuasion.

Recent studies indicate that the average leader spends 70% of his working day with the skills of communication, be it writing, reading, speaking, or listening. When describing the ideal man, Aristotle mentioned "a deep voice and a deliberate way of speaking."

The leader must be persuasive. Unfortunately, many people feel that persuasion is akin to manipulation and propaganda. Many associate persuasion with high-pressure salesmanship. Some Christians believe that every aspect of persuasion should be the work of the Holy Spirit. The Holy Spirit works on man by reason, argument, and motive. A Divine persuasion can only excite and draw out the strength we have, delivering the mind and affections from prejudices and other moral impediments.

"The mind of the wise makes his speech judicious, and adds persuasiveness to his lips" (Prov. 16:23). Paul argued and persuaded Jews and Greeks (Acts 18:4), he spoke boldly, arguing and pleading about the kingdom of God, trying to convince people (Acts 18:4; 19:8; 28:23). Some were convinced, others disbelieved. He was not universally successful. The seed must fall into good ground. There must be receptivity. The listener is not passive, an inert lump. The word "receptivity" covers a wide scale.

We speak of a host *receiving* his friends. This kind of *reception* is entirely different from that of a vessel which is filled with an alien substance. In the former sense, receiving is participation. In this sense it is an act and an art . . . like that of the host who brings out the best in his guest and creates a genuine communication and exchange. The communication is received, actively entertained, as a host receives his friend. This goes far beyond propaganda or publicity. This is effective communication.

Communication has been defined as the arousal by a signal of some kind of some degree of common perception among two or more individuals. It has been suggested that communication is a serious address and response between two or more persons, in which the being and truth of each is confronted by the being and truth of the other. A simple and convenient way to describe an act of communication is to answer the following questions: *Who* says *what,* through *which* channel, to *whom,* with what *effect?* Attention is focused on the communicator, the communication, the methodology, the receiver, and the result.

The first difficulty is with the person of the communicator. When a man sets himself to speak, he does so because he believes he will be able to say what he thinks. This is perhaps an illusion because language is not quite up to that. We always say more or less what we think and in the process of speech we raise an obstacle to the full transmission of our thought. It is necessary to leave some things unsaid in order to say others, because everything would be unsayable.

The communicator must be a source of valid assertions. Trustworthiness and expertness are two essential factors in intelligent communication. Communication cannot be exhaustive, but it must be adequate. "No saying says of itself all it wants to say. It says a small fraction and the rest is implied and taken as a matter of course. This defectiveness is congenital to language. If in speaking we had to say all we need to say so as to preclude ambiguity, language would be impossible. What we actually convey is dependent on innumerable things that remain silent. Language exists through the possibility of reticence, and what is communicated lives on that which is left unsaid and taken for granted. The tacit supplement, which by far outweighs the explicit part of any sentence, is put across in various ways, above all through that which has been said before and that which follows. Every text presents itself as a fragment of a context. Every text and context in their turn presuppose and allude to a situation out of which has arisen what is actually said. This situation is ultimately inexpressible."[31]

Because of limitations of formal communication the Christian leader may find it desirable to engage in casual and nonpurposive conversations.

Communication must be meaningful to the group or else it will be considered improbable, remote, unimportant, or unapplicable. For this reason the leader has to ask himself: Who should know

[31]Ortega y Gasset, *Concord and Liberty* (N.Y., W. W. Norton & Co.), 1946, p. 98.

about this? Does this information relate to this person? How much of the information I possess does the other person need to know? Is this the right moment for sharing the information?

In the process of communication there are always several elements: What I intend to say, what I really say, what the other person hears, what the other person thinks he hears, how the other person responds and what I think the other person says. The possibilities of distortion are enormous.

Good communication does not necessarily mean that the point of persuasion has been reached. It simply means that the other person understands the message clearly.

At the same time the leader will have to organize persuasive arguments for maximum effectiveness. This will largely depend on the education and composition of the group with which he is working. It is the task of the leader to study the various factors involved in order to achieve persuasive communication.

Paul denied his own idiosyncrasies in order to become all things to all men and to reach them effectively. He made himself a slave to all—served them all by teaching in word and deed—in order to win some. At the same time he never tried to please men by denying the content of the gospel. His goal was clear and unmistakable—the communication of the gospel—and so he endeavored to persuade. To this end he was willing to adapt himself to all men in order to reach some. At Antioch he spoke to the Jews and reviewed the history of Israel culminating in the Messiah. At Athens, facing a pagan audience, he quoted from pagan poets—but the central message was always the same.

Leaders must study and use the art of communication since they are called to teach and train. It is fascinating to study the methods Christ used to communicate with men and women of different walks of life or with the Twelve, the disciples, and the crowd.

To know where truth lies is not more important than knowing how to deliver it. Men govern with words, and battles are won through their ability to express concrete ideas in clear and unmistakable language. The speeches Churchill made during the difficult months of 1940 mobilized the British nation and electrified the world. The words of Mao Tse-tung have galvanized China and exercised enormous influence.

The Greek term for persuasion implies the idea of creating confidence. In a Mayan language spoken in Guatemala by the Conobs, the phrase used to express persuasion is extremely personal and intimate in its implications. It literally means "to give one's soul to." If one persuades another, he figuratively "gives his soul to him." Real, lasting, and effective persuasion must involve this giving process. This is in direct conflict with modern propaganda imposing itself on the mind. The persuasion of the Scripture gives itself to the heart and soul.

Since the average person is exposed to a barrage of communication, response has been dulled. It becomes an even greater challenge to the leader to communicate adequately and persuasively.

The desire to communicate is one of the leadership traits. The word "expression" is derived from two Latin words: *ex* and *premere*. It is well known that *ex* means "out of," whereas *premere* means "to press," as one would press the fruit to extract the juice. Two ideas are reflected in the word "expression"—the notion of strength or pressure and the concept of projecting toward the outside. Several elements are involved: the leader who is expressing himself; the internal pressure which compels him to express and to communicate; the projection toward the outside; the effectiveness of that which is projected and the one who receives the expression.

Communication is one of the vital links between the leader and the group. It may be symbolic or verbal, direct or indirect, frequent or sporadic, but it must be clear and adequate and lead to reception and participation. Communication must flow from the deep desire of the leader to share, to involve others, to teach and to train, to precede and to lead. What Paul wrote centuries ago to the Thessalonians in his very first letter remains true: "So you became our followers . . . for you received our messages" (I Thess. 1:6 LNT).

8

The Cost of Leadership

Loneliness

If the leader is defined as walking ahead of the group, he is necessarily separated from the group, alone, isolated. It is in this sense that H. Ellis wrote: To be a leader one must turn one's back on men. At the same time the full weight of responsibility rests on the leader. Joseph Conrad, in *Typhoon,* describes the situation well: "Jukes was uncritically glad to have his captain at hand. It relieved him as though that man had, by simply coming on deck, taken most of the gale's weight upon his shoulders. Such is the prestige, the privilege, and the burden of command. Captain MacWhirr could expect no relief of that sort from any one on earth. Such is the loneliness of command."

In a sense the leader has lost his freedom in the service of others. He promotes their interests, articulates their values, and defines their goals. At the same time he fulfills his own potential and is not absorbed by the group. This is a delicate balance which ultimately leaves the leader alone. After all, unoriginal followers can hardly appreciate original leadership.

Learning has been described as a process of contact and withdrawal. From the standpoint of leadership one might speak of identification with and isolation from the group. Both are necessary.

In Elijah we find a combination of contemplative solitude and dynamic action. Moments of isolation permitting meditation and reflection are followed by a return to the task with renewed vigor. The leader is not a hermit, but he must be an individuality. Solitude may be combined with genuine universality, with ecumenical consciousness. Solitude is not to be equated with individualism or alienation. Solitude is compatible with universality.

In one sense Christ was solitary. He was not understood during his life. He was deserted—and every act of courage and every creative initiative tends to isolate the leader.

Some people cannot function without a crowd. At one point in his life Jesus "sent away the people" (Mk. 6:45). It is a great art, that of being able to leave a crowd. Jesus did not depend on the deceptive presence of a throng. He could walk away from it. He could leave it when something more central, more vital, more permanent called. He left the crowd to go up into the hills to pray, to minister to one or two, rather than to be surrounded by five thousand.

Are we able to leave a crowd in our personal lives? There are many who can collect a crowd, but cannot do the harder thing, collect *themselves.* Their life is as public as the waiting room of a railway station. To some a milling crowd is a necessary shot in the arm, without which life languishes; but without solitude there can be no fine singularity, only a chaotic plural. There cannot be opportunity for what J. A. Bengel called "leisure for building up myself in the recollected consciousness of God. Jesus' whole life makes it clear that what we can bring of worth to any crowd depends on whether we can leave it."[1] The ability to withdraw must be balanced by the facility to communicate with the group.

Identification—Isolation

The leader can never be seen in abstraction, but only in relation to the group. If he stands at the head, goes before, is the first,

---

[1]*The Interpreters Bible* (Nashville, Tenn., Abingdon Press), 1951, Vol. 7, on Mark 4:36.

takes the helm, or holds the reins—whatever metaphor may be used, a group is implied.

The leader walks ahead of the group and this implies distance. Distance, in turn, creates tension. This is one of the crucial aspects of leadership. How far dare the leader be in advance of the group? He can stretch the distance . . . move out of sight and lose his following. Conversely, he can be "one of the boys," identify with the group, diminish distance and even eradicate it. Isolation or identification?

There must always be some distance between the leader and the followers. The very notion of leadership involves precedence. The leader walks ahead of the group as Jesus on the way to Jerusalem was walking ahead of his disciples; "and they were amazed, and those who followed were afraid. And taking the Twelve again, he began to tell them what was to happen to him" (Mk. 10:32).

The Master was unafraid, certain, steadfast. He walked in advance of the Twelve with solemnity and determination. His manner struck awe into the minds of the Twelve, who were beginning at last to anticipate an impending disaster. The rest of the company, the crowd which usually hung upon the Lord's footsteps, were conscious of vague fear. There was a risk of real panic and the Lord checked his course until the Twelve had come up to him. He admitted them again to his company. He would not permit too great a distance between himself and the disciples, at least not to the point of real panic.

To be effective, the leader cannot be too far in advance, or at variance with the general view of his group . . . at least, not if he wishes to remain the leader and to remain effective. This pragmatic aspect of leadership may collide with deep-seated convictions. It may not be easy to create a platform sufficiently familiar in trend and temper to be sympathetically received. If the discrepancy between the vision of the leader and of the group as to what is good is too pronounced, if the concept of the leader as to the goal and the method to reach the goal does not coincide with the purpose and aspiration of the group, tension will build between the leader and the followers.

When the disciples followed with amazement and the crowd

with fear, Jesus stopped and took the Twelve into his confidence. He identified with the group. In another situation he had no alternative but to say to the Twelve: Will you also go away? At the basis of identification is love. Paul had great sorrow and unceasing anguish in his heart for his kinsmen by race and wished that he were cut off from Christ for their sake. He became a Jew to the Jews. Jesus was moved with compassion when he saw the multitude, and wept over Jerusalem. His incarnation was the greatest act of identification. He partook of the same nature and was made like unto his brethren. He suffered and was tempted. His identification was complete. Yet, he was without sin—the distance between Christ and mankind was extraordinary, as vast as between holiness and sin, heaven and earth, light and darkness. The resulting tension was inevitable.

If, in a certain sense, the leader must belong to the group, it is also true that he must never merge into the group to the extent where position and status are submerged, or where he ceases to represent the ideal. He is sociable, friendly, and helpful, but not necessarily an intimate friend of each or any of the members of the group. On the other hand, it is also true, that "men who meet only for definite serious purposes, and on official occasions, do not wholly meet. They may have some common concern very much at heart; they may, in the course of repeated contacts, come to share a vocabulary and an idiom which appear to communicate every shade of meaning necessary for their common purpose; but they will continue to retire from these encounters each to his private social world as well as to his solitary world . . . it is unfortunate for a man when his friends and his business associates are two unrelated groups; it is also narrowing when they are one and the same group."[2]

Much has been written in recent years about the "I-Thou" relationship, although few may have read and understood Martin Buber. He speaks of "I-Thou" as primary words, spoken from the being, establishing the world of relation. The "I-Thou" relationship is one of openness, directness, mutuality and presence. It may take place between man and man, but also with a tree, a cat, a fragment of mica, or a work of art.

[2]T. S. Eliot, *Christianity and Culture* (N.Y., Harcourt, Brace & World), 1949, p. 160.

Martin Buber wrote: "The true community does not arise through peoples' having feelings for one another (though indeed not without it), but through, first, their taking their stand in living mutual relationship with a living Centre, and second, their being in living mutual relation with one another. The second has its source in the first, but is not given when the first alone is given. Living mutual relationship includes feelings, but does not originate with them. The community is built up out of living relations, but the builder is the living effective Centre."[3] If *Jesus* is substituted for *Centre,* then this paragraph expresses the relationship of a Christian group to Christ and to the leader. Leadership involves interaction between the group and the leader, as well as between members of the group.*

Bonhoeffer's emphasis differed: "Unless we have the courage to fight for a revival of a wholesome reserve between man and man, all human values will be submerged in anarchy . . . our duty today . . . is basically to defend the sense of reserve between man and man. We shall be accused of acting for our own interests, of being anti-social . . .".[4] This thought is echoed by Harvey Cox when he writes that "human beings cannot bear to have 'I-Thou' relationships in all their connections with the various worlds of modern life. Urban man must be selective. He is exposed to so many different people that he must cultivate the 'personal' qualities in some and discourage them in others."[5] Elsewhere he expresses the thought that "aside from the 'I-it' relationship where the other person is reduced to an object, and in addition to the very profound and personal 'I-Thou' relationship, one should perhaps consider an 'I-you' relationship. It would include all those public relationships we so enjoy in the city but which we do not allow to develop into private ones. These contacts can be decidedly human

---

*It is interesting that Freud was unable to work with the group he had established. "I could not succeed in establishing among the members those friendly relations that ought to obtain between men who are all engaged upon the same difficult work, nor could I crush out the disputes about priority for which there were many opportunities under these conditions of work in common."

[3]Martin Buber, *I and Thou* (N.Y., Charles Scibner's Sons), 1958, p. 45.

[4]Dietrich Bonhoeffer, *Letters and Papers from Prison* (N.Y., Macmillan), 1962, p. 28.

[5]Harvey Cox, *The Secular City* (N.Y., Macmillan Co.), 1965, pp. 172, 48–49.

even though they remain somewhat distant." One might perhaps speak of functional relationships.

In the same vein, Hamilton writes that reserve "also means a willingness to leave the other person alone, to let him be himself, apart from us . . . There must be a genuine space between man and man, lest, seeing so clearly the dangers of destroying another by arrogance and hostility, we find ourselves destroying him by love, forgiveness, or acceptance. Thus, reserve means respect for the other's right to solitariness, and a defense both for ourselves and for the other of the rights of privacy and solitude. Respect means giving the other the full right to be apart from us, apart from society, alone."[6]

These thoughts are of particular significance to the leader in relation to the group. He is always in search of balance, ahead of the group without producing unbearable tension, close to the group without permitting total identification. All possible relationships, including 'I-Thou,' 'I-it,' or 'I-you,' intimate, impersonal, or functional, become a part of his daily existence and are largely dictated by the situation in which he finds himself, or the expectation of the group.

It is difficult to define the degree of identification or isolation. This will largely depend on the task and the type of leadership required to accomplish it. General George C. Marshall often stated that the top man should not be too close to the men working with and for him. This may be necessary for military men who must protect themselves from the emotional impact of ordering friends into battle and maybe into death. A Secretary of State may develop a different philosophy because of the different setting. Not one member of Lincoln's cabinet was a personal friend or even follower of the President.

If the leader merely voices the aspirations of the group, if he experiences their emotions and senses their moods, if leadership is essentially interpretation, a reading of common thought, if the main weapon of the leader is charm and if he leads his followers like an actor leads his audience, then identification should be as complete as possible. The redemptive leader may

[6]William Hamilton, *New Essence of Christianity* (N.Y., Association Press), 1966, p. 124.

have a different viewpoint. His may be a clearer vision, a broader perspective, a greater concept. He may fully understand the conscious needs of the group, but cherish higher ambitions, loftier goals and more elevated principles for the group. He may, at times, be compelled to walk alone and to share the experience of Elijah who said: I, even I only am left; and they seek my life to take it away. This experience of despondency followed a wave of temporary popular acclaim. At one point the Psalmist felt solitary like the vulture of the wilderness, like an owl of the waste place. His isolation was involuntary and accompanied with a deep craving for fellowship. In this respect, the experience of Jesus at Gethsemane is unique and unforgettable.

Regardless of the style of leadership adopted, as long as leadership is maintained, a certain tension will come into play. Not every conflict is necessarily neurotic. Some is normal and healthy. The tension between what is and what ought to be—the gap between reality and ideal—is indispensable to well-being. Every challenge carries tension within itself. We do not need a tension-less state, but a challenging goal and purpose.

The redemptive leader may feel that the voice of the people is not always the voice of God! Moses could seldom yield to the demands of the people. He desired redemption, true liberty for the nation and was compelled to refuse their irrational (or very rational) demands. It takes courage to say 'no' to followers and to lose popularity.

If the distance between the leader and the group is exaggerated, he may lose his position of leadership altogether—although he may still be a leader in a different category, a leader in thought, a pioneer, misunderstood because he is so far ahead of his time. The music of Bach was only appreciated years after his death. We should never despise the lone musing of the genius. He may not be a team-leader, but still a leader of supreme significance.

To some extent the leader always generates resentment. It has been called "positional resentment." The mere fact that there is a leader focuses resentment upon him. In the case of the entrepreneur resentment is balanced by admiration. This is why he escapes open resentment which comes down like an avalanche upon his successor.

In this context it is interesting to study the relationship of Jesus with the crowd, the disciples, and the Twelve. He was often compelled to refuse the crowd's requests. In answer to a foolish interpellation, revealing an egotistical disposition, the words of Jesus are sternly repressive: "Man, who made me a judge or divider over you?" The word "man" echoes thorough disapprobation and a desire to stand aloof (Lk. 12:13,14). Nor could Jesus grant the request of James and John regarding the first places at his left and right.

At times he condescended to answer foolish questions arising from the crowd or even the disciples and showed great patience and tenderness at every step. But gradually, he lost his popularity and the number of followers shrunk. At a given time even many of his disciples drew back and no longer went with him.

Jesus persevered in his service, i.e. his teaching. He could not compromise. His goal was too important, his conviction too strong. Jesus could not always accede to the demands of the Twelve although they were his closest friends and followers. Even John was rebuked at times. The redemptive leader may have to follow the footsteps of the Master and walk in solitude. This has been the experience of many leaders throughout the history of the church, from the early "Fathers" such as Chrysostom or Athanasius to our own day.

Since many goals cannot be reached in isolation, the group is essential. The leader may have to make temporary concessions and lead graciously and progressively without losing sight of the long-range objective. Each one will have to face this issue and the true leader will find the necessary balance.

The Balance

The profile of a leader is that of a person with the desire to lead, willing to accept responsibility, equipped with courage and competence, sensitive and sympathetic, enthusiastic but emotionally stable, realistic but imaginative, creative, intelligent, decisive, endowed with endurance, tact, and humor. Above all, the profile of a leader should be that of a sincere willingness to serve because of genuine concern, inspired by divine love, ever and always conscious of the ultimate goal—to be redemptive, to serve Jesus Christ.

There is not one perfect life in the gallery of the great, except the life of our Lord Jesus Christ. The Christian leader will not necessarily possess all of the qualities enumerated but he will have some in more than average measure. In a deeper sense it is true that the world does not know him and does not understand the motivation of the Christian leader (1 Jn. 3:1). There is an element of inscrutability arousing curiosity and creating suspense.

The Christian leader is not determined by uncontrolled impulses. The fruit of the Spirit is self-control (Gal. 5:23), temperance, the mastery of all appetites and passions. This self-control regulates the expression of energy and maintains the balance of the personality. The skill of the serpent and the simplicity of the dove are combined. The character is balanced.

The Christian leader is able to resist praise, contrary to those who "receive glory" from one another and do not seek the glory that comes from the only God" (Jn. 5:44). The redemptive leader is not determined by earthly ambitions. He is not afraid to break with the spirit of the age. He is not among those who love "the praise of men more than the praise of God" (Jn. 12:43). The Christian leader knows that "the fear of man lays a snare" (Prov. 29:25), and will not allow the judgment of man to become his standard.

The leader is a disciple. Day after day he listens as a disciple, as one who is taught of God in order to sustain with a word those who are weary, in order to have a message to communicate to those who are his followers (Isa. 50:4,5). As a disciple he seeks only the glory that comes from God. Selfish striving after personal honor no longer predominates. In the ultimate sense this would exclude the love of God and make faith impossible. The appeal of Christ was not to the eye but to the heart; not to the outward, but to the inward; not to the temporal, but to the eternal. The Christian leader may face disapprobation and disappointment, but such experiences only arouse new creative thoughts and stimulate new efforts, furnish new insights, strengthen desire, and renew dedication. It is true that in some sense the leader might prefer to live quietly as a private person, but he is compelled to act daringly and boldly. He is constrained by the love of God, by the love which flows from God, molds him and drives him on. He is convinced that his capacities await development and expression because they are not his private possession. He is not his own. The world will not understand the hidden springs of his action. The outsiders do not understand his principles, his methods, and his character, for the true knowledge of man requires sympathy. Although different situations will demand more or fewer of the qualities mentioned, the Christian leader is deeply conscious that the *spring of action* is given simply by the fact that he has experienced redemption through Jesus Christ. In turn, he then wishes to be redemptive in word and deed. The Christian leader, like the Son of man, is motivated by love to serve others in order to lead them to the freedom which will enable them to become what they ought to be.

9

The Leader and the Group

It is impossible to speak of the leader without taking the group into consideration. If the leader is one who walks ahead of the group, then the latter is of utmost importance, since without followers, leadership evaporates. In fact, leadership has been defined in terms of the group, as the process of arranging a situation so that various members of the group, including the leader, can achieve common goals with maximum economy and a minimum of time and work. The leader is accepted because he helps his followers fulfill their aspirations and realize their dreams.

Ever since the *leadership traits* theory became unfashionable, the pendulum swung in the opposite direction and almost exclusive attention has been focused on the group. Now the leader is portrayed not in terms of his personality, but in his functional relationship to the group in specific situations. He emerges to achieve the objective desired by the group. The group is using the leader to attain their objectives. This concept is not altogether new. Melville wrote: "I always go to sea as a sailor, because of the wholesome exercise and pure air of the forecastle deck. For as in this world, head winds are far more prevalent than winds from astern (that is, if you never violate the Pythagorean maxim), so for the most part the Commodore on the quarter-deck gets his atmosphere at second hand from the sailors on the forecastle. He thinks he breathes it first; but not so. In much the same way do the commonality lead their leaders in many other things, at the same time the leaders little suspect it."[7] In the same vein Eric Hoffer writes in *The True Believer:* "In a free society the leader follows the people even as he leads them. He must, as someone said, find out where the people are going so that he may lead them. When the leader in a free society becomes contemptuous of the people, he sooner or later proceeds on the false and fatal theory that all man are fools, and eventually blunders into defeat."[8]

The emphasis on group effectiveness and group dynamics has been particularly strong in the United States. It is the unavoidable reflection of a more democratic, more participative, more permissive and non-directive environment.

In the interest of semantic clarity it is necessary to distinguish community from society and fellowship from a group. There is a fundamental distinction between *community,* which is related to an organic, deep-seated, emotionally persuasive and genuine form of being together, over against *society,* which is a more mechanical association, temporary and artificial. A *group* has been defined as a unit composed of two or more organism with a collective perception of its unity, interacting and pursuing a common goal. Perhaps it is easiest to define a group as a "number of individuals assembled together or having common interests."

The relation between leader and group is largely determined by the expectation and situation of the group. The relation can be leader-centered or group-centered, depending on the measure of authority in the hands of the leader or the freedom and maturity of the group. Regardless of the specific situation, the leader always has a two-fold responsibility to the group:

1. He functions to meet the need of the group at the working level. Groups have definite tasks, objectives to reach. The leader facilitates the group effort by furnishing definitions, and assigning specific tasks; by requesting facts and seeking information—or by furnishing the data. He synthesizes, summarizes, clarifies, and restates.

---

[7]Herman Melville, *Moby Dick* (N.Y., Collier Books), 1962, p. 34.
[8]*Idem.,* p. 110.

2. Any group experiences constantly changing interactions and relationships within itself. Group dynamics differ in every group, each one presenting a unique pattern of forces. It is part of the leadership function to increase the self-awareness of the group and to strengthen interpersonal relationships. What is at stake here is group loyalty and mutual loyalty. The perceptive leader senses group feelings and moods, reconciles disagreements, reduces tension, keeps communication channels open and infuses a genuine spirit of fellowship. Although theoretically this should be far easier in a Christian group, *it ain't necessarily so!*

To achieve this, the leader needs to know something of the nature of the group, the history, previous experience, personal attitudes of the members, group cohesion and atmosphere. He who would ride horseback must know the horse's nature, respect it, and work carefully with it. He who would sail in a storm must adapt himself to the wind and the waves as if he were a part of them. The leader must gain the mastery by understanding the nature of the men he leads and thus without violating that nature the leader achieves his purpose.

Group Dynamics

Group dynamics is the driving spiritual, moral, or intellectual force of a specific group. It is evident in every meeting that each group has its own peculiar dynamic. Group dynamics describes the interaction within the group—the interpersonal relationships. It refers to the problem of communication and describes the manner in which decisions are reached.

Two factors must be taken into consideration: Group cohesiveness, i.e. the attractiveness of the group for the members, and also the satisfaction of individual needs. These four elements of group dynamics—*communication, decision-making, cohesiveness* and *individual needs*—play a major role and must be considered.

Communication

Aside from goal orientation and a precise definition of the task, it is essential for each group to achieve a high degree of communication among its members. Operationally it is difficult for a group to speak or act except through individual members. If everyone talks at once, no one can hear. If everyone plans at once, or acts at once without a plan, group action evaporates and nothing remains but a collection of individuals planning or acting. For a group to act as a unit it is necessary that individuals speak for it. This demands a certain group structure, an internal arrangement in order to avoid çonfusion and uncertainty. Without such safeguards the weaker members of the group will be overwhelmed.

Almost everything that has been said regarding communication as it affects the leader, could be repeated in this context. The free flow of communication is particularly important in group dynamics. It must be possible for each member of the group to express himself freely, even when his viewpoint differs from the one entertained by the group. Without such a free flow of ideas much will remain latent and never come to the forefront. It is therefore particularly important to establish good communication channels, both formal and informal.

The ineffectiveness of groups has been castigated in *The Fountainhead:*

> Kent Lansing smiled. "Have you ever known a board to do anything?"
> "What do you mean?"
> "Just that: have you ever known a board to do anything at all?"
> "Well, they seem to exist and function."
> "Do they? You know, there was a time when everyone thought it self-evident that the earth was flat. It would be entertaining to speculate upon the nature and causes of humanity's illusions. I'll write a book about it some day. It won't be popular. I'll have a chapter on boards of directors. You see, they don't exist."
> "I'd like to believe you, but what's the gag?"
> "No, you wouldn't like to believe me. The causes of illusions are not pretty to discover. They're either vicious or tragic. This one is both. Mainly vicious. And it's not a gag. But we won't go into that now. All I mean is that a board of directors is one or two ambitious men—and a lot of ballast. I mean that groups of men are vacuums. Great big empty nothings. They say we can't visualize a total nothing. Hell, sit at any committee

meeting. The point is only who chooses to fill that nothing. It's a tough battle. The toughest. It's simple enough to fight any enemy, so long as he's there to be fought. But when he isn't . . . Don't look at me like that, as if I were crazy. You ought to know. You've fought a vacuum all your life."[9]

But a board or a group is not a vacuum. This description is a caricature—which does not mean that the picture is impossible, only that hopefully it is unlikely.

One of the key problems of any group is the difficulty of self-criticism and self-evaluation. This was one of the great problems of the Middle Ages when those who advocated measures of reform within the Catholic Church hoped that they could be achieved through a general council. It was expecting too much to hope that a council would make drastic changes, when it was made up of men profiting by the abuses it was supposed to eliminate. These efforts failed. The danger always subsists that criticism will be stifled, negative communication cut off, and dissenters silenced.

Since a group cannot function without some structure—be it ever so minimal—and since some members have more status than others, good group interaction is not as easy to achieve as might be assumed. To establish meaningful dialogue, to communicate effectively remains a challenging problem.

Without such freedom of communication, the group becomes as much of a tyrant as the despot it supposedly replaced. The group can become as authoritarian as an individual leader. Emphasis on agreement may inhibit creativity. The group concept should not be allowed to degenerate to the point where anyone with a different philosophy or a different ethos does not fit.

In reality people very rarly *think* in groups; they talk together, they exchange information, they adjudicate, they make compromises, but they do not think; they do not create. Someone must take the necessary initiative; a structure has to be developed for communication. It is obviously true that if every member simply wants to do what the entire group wishes to do, then the group is not going to do anything.

---

[9]*Op. cit.,* p. 312.

Decision-making

Some group members have a very low threshold of basic security. Almost any relationship with another person—even the most harmless one—threatens to overwhelm them. This explains the weakness of group action, or group decision when the majority of the group is composed of such persons. In any group meeting, every participant is exposed to the total impact of all the stimuli present. This group atmosphere is often highly charged. Aside from direct verbal communication there is significant non-verbal communication, both consciously and unconsciously in posture, facial expression, and gesture. Group tension can build fast and generate talk. Language is used as a substitute for action in order to discharge tension. This vicarious use of language communicates little and clarifies nothing. It does reduce tension, but does not lead to a decision.

The decision-making abilities of a group vary considerably depending on the nature of the leadership, the task orientation of the group, and the existential situation. We have already considered different styles of leadership which would have direct bearing on the decision-making process. Groups always operate within a certain set of procedures. Normally there is an agenda, topics to be discussed. The structure of the discussion has to be appropriate to the size of the group and the task to be accomplished. This does not mean that everything has to be formalized. Procedures are seldom explicitly spelled out but tacitly accepted and understood by the group members.

Group decisions are not easily reached. All too often it is true that "those who see their lives as spoiled and wasted crave equality and fraternity more than they do freedom. If they clamor for freedom, it is but freedom to establish equality and uniformity. The passion for equality is partly a passion for anonymity."[10] At this point the search for excellence is abandoned in favor of uniformity in the name of democracy and equality. Does group action compel the group member to abandon individual excellence in favor of mass mediocrity?

---

[10]Eric Hoffer, *The True Believer* (N.Y., Harper & Row), 1966, p. 37.

Equalitarianism

In a democratic system men have equal rights, but it does not follow that they have equal ability. It is a crude notion to equate equality with sameness. The notion of equality can become so coercive that sameness seems to be the only social virtue. Group unanimity is paramount. Such tyranny inhibits communication.

Some school children have demanded less than the best of themselves for fear of the unpopularity that goes with the desire to excel. The same may hold true for an individual in a group. All too often equality means sameness, rather than oneness. At the same time it must be recognized that people want to conform to a much higher degree than they are compelled to conform, at least in the western democracies.

Group unity is important, but it is dangerous to generate unification through reduction, through the loss of differences which confer on group members their distinctiveness and value. Reduction is achieved through the obliteration of specific characteristics in order to produce uniformity. This automatically leads to impoverishment of the entire group.

Not all the members of the group contribute equally to the well-being of the group. Some bring to it much more. Men are not equal in their native gifts, neither in their motivations nor in their achievements. Gifted people are more highly valued and therefore permitted a greater degree of nonconformity. Persons of high prestige are freer not to conform should they so desire. Weaker persons in the group may feel that they can develop a sense of belonging only if they conform to existing norms. For that matter, even some persons of large influence may really feel that their status depends upon conformity with group norms rather than upon their contribution to the group.

According to Will Durant: "Inequality is not only natural and inborn, it grows with the complexity of civilization. Hereditary inequalities breed social and artificial inequalities; every invention or discovery is made or seized by the exceptional individual, and makes the strong stronger, the weak relatively weaker, than before.

Economic development specializes functions, differentiates abilities, and makes men unequally valuable to their group . . . Even when repressed, inequality grows; only the man who is below average in economic ability desires equality; those who are conscious of superior ability desire freedom; and in the end superior ability has its way."[11]

Along the same line Arthur M. Schlesinger, Jr. writes that "Modern democracy inadvertently gave envy a new scope. While the purpose of democracy was to give everyone a fair chance to rise, its method enabled rancorous men to envoke 'equality' as an excuse for keeping all down to their own level."[12]

From a different vantage point, David Riesman in *The Lonely Crowd* concludes: "The idea that men are created free and equal is both true and misleading: men are created different; they lose their social freedom and their individual autonomy in seeking to become like each other."[13]

C. S. Lewis, looking at the problem from a Christian perspective in *The Weight of Glory,* writes with characteristic insight: "And now I must say something that may appear to you a paradox. You have often heard that, though in the world we hold different stations, yet we are equal in the sight of God. There are of course senses in which this is true. God is no accepter of persons: his love for us is not measured by our social rank or our intellectual talents. But I believe there is a sense in which this maxim is the reverse of the truth. I am going to venture to say that artificial equality is necessary in the life of the State, but that in the Church we strip off this disguise, we recover our real inequalities and are thereby refreshed and quickened.

"I believe in political equality. But there are two opposite reasons for being a democrat. You may think all men so good that they deserve a share in the government of the commonwealth, and so wise that the commonwealth needs their advice. That is, in my opinion, the false, romantic doctrine of democracy. On the

---

[11]Will Durant, *The Lessons of History* (N.Y., Simon & Schuster), 1968, p. 20.

[12]Arthur Schlesinger, Jr., "Greatness," *Saturday Evening Post,* Nov. 1, 1958.

[13]David Riesman, *The Lonely Crowd* (New Haven, Yale University Press), 1950, p. 373.

other hand, you may believe fallen men to be so wicked that not one of them can be trusted with any irresponsibile power over his fellows. That I believe to be the true ground of democracy."[14]

"Extreme equalitarianism—or, as I would prefer to say, *equalitarianism wrongly conceived*—which ignores differences in native capacity and achievement, has not served democracy well. Carried far enough, it means the lopping off of any heads which come above dead level. It means committee rule, the individual smothered by the group. And it means the end of that striving for excellence which has produced mankind's greatest achievements."[15]

As Berdyaev expresses it: "Equality is an evil when in its name high qualities are destroyed and the greatness of individuality is rejected. A consistent metaphysic of democratism is profoundly hostile to every high calling and to all true greatness. This is the metaphysic of the plain, afraid of anything that is of the heights or of exaltation. The metaphysic of democratism resists all elements of genius and rejects the leadership of greatness. In its view, power in the world belongs to some mechanism of quantity, not to the highly qualified individual but to the average and the ordinary. Democratism exerts itself to make quality subject to quantity, the individual to the general, the great to the average. But every value is qualitative, individual, of the heights. Hence the value of equality in democratic metaphysics is hostile to all true values."[16] These words are a warning against the technology anxious to standardize man to the point where he might become interchangeable. The concept of the group, the cohesive unit, must be balanced by an emphasis on the individual as a person. It is this dynamic tension between the person and the group which becomes creative and productive.

Over against a mistaken notion of equalitarianism stands the challenge of excellence. It was Paul's prayer for the Philippians that they might "prove what is excellent." Smugness and self-satisfaction are enemies of excellence, resulting in mediocrity and

[14]C. S. Lewis, *The Weight of Glory* (N.Y., MacMillan), 1949, p. 36.
[15]John W. Gardner, *Excellence* (N.Y., Harper & Row), 1961, p. 15.
[16]Nicolas Berdyaev, *The Meaning of the Creative Act* (N.Y., Collier Books), 1962, pp. 262–267.

failure. Excellence arises from unceasing efforts to do better. Excellence is related to values and ideals rather than expertise. The pursuit of excellence raises the question: What do I consider to be the highest good toward which all my efforts should direct themselves?

Excellence is not merely skill in taking examinations, following instructions, or finding solutions. This type of excellence can be learned by well-developed techniques. One should never confuse academic ability with excellence. For that matter, there are many talents which can hardly be measured or quantified, such as artistic talent. But excellence is still found in a different realm. The excellent man makes great demands on himself. His life is marked by consistent and redemptive service. He has found freedom in service. The necessity of serving is not felt as an oppression. Should the necessity be removed, he would be restless and invent a new standard, more difficult, more exigent with which to coerce himself. It is a life lived in discipline, a noble life . . . and nobility is defined by the demands that it makes upon us.

Unfortunately we have focused increasingly on a single type of excellence—on practical results, on the tangible. Our society is action oriented. The reward of successful leadership is more leadership—all too often equated with hyperactivity. Leisure is available only to the unsuccessful. What is most admired is triumphant talent, success, be it in athletics, art, or business. It is *always* activistic. The significance of leisure has been overlooked and the lone musings of genius which do not fall into the time schedule and way of life of the businessman are disregarded. More place must be given to the creative and reflective faculties over against activism. The biblical emphasis on meditation needs to be learned anew.

Group norms must be sufficiently flexible to permit the pursuit of excellence. The decision-making process should not rule out dynamic tension, or encourage unanimity at the expense of individuality. Equalitarianism wrongly conceived should not threaten the creative person in the group. On the other hand, a group is more than just a collection of individuals. Togetherness is not enough. There must be coalescence, a fusing and blending into a compact whole. To achieve this, communication channels must be open, the decision-making process dynamic, and a balance must be maintained between equality and excellence.

Cohesiveness

The word "group" speaks of cohesiveness. In order to become part of a compact whole the individual has to forego something. We have already seen that it may not be easy to maintain a balance between group cohesion and individual freedom. Functionally, fellowship has been defined as working together as a group toward a common goal. It is not merely being together, but working together. If each member has subordinate goals and if the group as a whole moves toward the total goal, then fellowship shall not stand in the way of efficiency. A frame of reference is needed for fellowship—a task orientation. Just as it would be most uncomfortable to be without ceiling, floor, and walls, so a framework of reference is needed to create cohesion, compactness. United action is the key. The group should not degenerate into an organized atrophy of personal existence.

Christian fellowship should result in an increasing unfolding of personality. Merely being together, far from binding, can result in a mere bundling together. A man in a crowd has been compared to a stick stuck in a bundle, moving through the water, abandoned to the current, or pushed by a pole from the bank in a given direction. Even if it seems to the stick that it is moving by its own motion, it has, in fact, none of its own; the bundle in which it drifts has only an illusion of self-propulsion.

In an organization, men are called upon to do something together. The group is not based on consanguinity, linguistic unity or territorial proximity. It is dynamic and animated by the will to do something in common—this is the essence of fellowship. There are always obstacles but these merely create the frontiers of outreach. Actually, they serve to consolidate the unification which already has been obtained. At first, obstacles loom large, but later they are viewed as means to strengthen group unity.

An organization is not built on extraneous principles, be they logical or geographic. It is not enough for an organization to have common glories in the past, to have done great things together, or to wish to do greater ones. For a group to exist, it is not enough to be able to look back upon a common past, because at one point the group was called into being and had no past. The common existence had to be created, and before it could be created there had to be a dream, a desire, a plan, and this purpose had to be fulfilled. If this purpose is frustrated, the group will not come into being or it will be abortive.

A group relies for its existence upon common consent in ultimate matters. This does not mean that nothing can be questioned, but the questioning is always related to minor divergencies and only serves to confirm and consolidate the underlying unanimity of the collective existence. If dissent affects the basic layers of common belief on which the solidarity of the group is resting, then it becomes a house divided and society dissociates, splitting up into two societies.

It should be far easier for Christians to achieve cohesion, since unity at the deepest level is created by the Holy Spirit. In reality this has not been true, and throughout the ages church history has been marked by divisions and factions. Some are mentioned in the New Testament, in apostolic days. The very fact that religious convictions are at stake may explain this lack of unity. Spiritual convictions run deep and seem to justify separations and disagreements. Frequently, theological reasons are invoked when in reality personality conflicts play the major role. It would be easy to illustrate this from almost any page of church history. Temperament, character, personality—all play a decisive role.

Because spiritual values are involved, cohesion may easily degenerate into pressure to conform. Detailed statements of faith are drawn up to safeguard group norms—but seldom prevent divisions. Monastic orders multiply—and oppose each other. Denominations increase—and fail to cooperate. Ethos prevails over excellence. Distinguishing character and tone, the correct pronunciation of shibboleth, is mistaken for fellowship and cohesiveness. All too often, criticism is silenced in the name of fellowship, uniformity confused with unity, togetherness substituted for action, and agreement misconstrued as oneness.

It is true that genuine cohesiveness rests upon the deepest Christian commitments to the person of Christ. It is essentially established by the Holy Spirit and tangibly manifested through concerted action.

A monolithic block lacks dynamic; a cohesive group submerges idiosyncrasies, maintains excellence, moves toward the goal accepted by the group, and is therefore task-oriented. Such cohesiveness produces satisfaction, generates a sense of belonging, and strengthens the group in its every effort.

Individual Needs

The apostolic group did not lack in diversity but maintained cohesion. They were always *the Twelve,* but within the ranks there was ample room for individuality. Jesus placed a tremendous emphasis on the individual, the one person, and it would have been surprising if he had tolerated unwholesome group uniformity.

Matthew had been a tax collector, working hand-in-hand with the hated Romans. Simon belonged to the Zealots, a fanatical Jewish party determined to liberate Israel from the yoke of the Roman oppressor. There was Peter, the enthusiast; Thomas, the logician; John, linked in warm friendship with Jesus; and Judas, the traitor. The contrasts were almost excessive, the personalities strongly marked. They were all part of *the Twelve,* members of a group.

There was a structure within the group. Three were always named first, and witnessed events from which the rest were excluded. At times, they worked two-by-two. Peter overshadowed his brother Andrew—although the latter had brought him to Jesus. At times there were discussions regarding preeminence and unavoidable jealousies. Through it all, *the Twelve* remained a cohesive group, and at the same time the individual needs of each member were met.

Usually there are far-reaching differences among men belonging to the same group. Characteristics vary from person to person. Physical and mental traits, emotional reactions, hereditary factors, environment and experience—all these elements shape personality. At the same time, there are some basic human needs at the root of behavior. Some of these needs are natural, physical needs such as those pertaining to food, drink, clothing, shelter, and the normal body functions. To satisfy these needs may become a goal, motivating the individual to behave in a specific manner.

Most needs are learned, acquired, and frequently determined by the social group in which we live and move. What is valued by someone else in his culture controls our behavior. Members of the peer group unconsciously project indirect goals to which we aspire. Perhaps three of the most basic individual needs and therefore of particular importance, are security, approval, and recognition.

Most people are anxious to avoid risks. They crave safety, they need assurance and guarantees. It may well be this desire to eliminate risk which led someone to join the group in the first place. It is easier, safer, to reach with and through the group. In this sense a group may meet an individual need.

Ortega y Gasset correctly analyzed the spring of mass action: "The question has been raised: How would a man of twenty today go about planning a life that would have a form peculiar to himself and that would therefore have to be realized by his own efforts and his own independent initiative? As he tries to unfold this picture in his mind, will he not become aware that if not impossible it is at least improbable, because there is no room for him to move according to the dictates of his own will? He will soon notice that his plan bumps against that of his neighbor, that his neighbor's life is pressing against his. With the ease of adaptation proper to his age, he will be driven by discouragement to give up not only all action but any personal desires as well, and will look for the opposite solution: he will imagine a standard life, made up of *desiderata* common to all, and he will realize that the only way of achieving it is to ask for it or demand it collectively with others."[17]

In his search for security, man joins a group. Within this group he may look for status, for approval, and recognition. In informal circles this may take the form of popularity. In more formal organizations, it may be seen in terms of earnings, responsibilities, etc. Men will put forth great efforts to win such approval. Few are willing to risk the disfavor of the group. Everyone wishes to

---

[17]Ortega y Gasset, *History as a System* (N.Y., W. W. Norton & Co.), 1962, p. 76.

retain a sense of belonging and participation. Without the latter, recognition is impossible. Most men feel the need for tangible proof that they are appreciated and needed.

When a new member joins a group, he must develop a feeling of belonging, of being part of the group. At first he may feel unimportant and tend to lose his sense of individuality. Strangely enough, sudden acceptance may sometimes lead to total release and thereby to uninhibited behavior.

Every new member, regardless of previous experience, requires an initial orientation and needs a warm and sincere reception. The newcomer is now disengaged from old moorings and the group needs to give him a fresh anchor, enabling him to feel secure once again. To the Christian, ultimate security comes from the Lord who is the foundation of life, but the Christian group will certainly demonstrate the redeeming love of God to the newcomer and strengthen him through the fellowship characteristic of the Christian faith.

It is the instinct of every living thing to persist in its own being. Change is resented and resisted. The group member with high status often opposes change in the mistaken assumption that his high prestige is due to strict conformity to group norms. The low-status member is zealous in group conformity to gain recognition as a loyal member, and therefore resists change. *The Ordeal of Change* is a provocative title and the opening paragraph strikingly true: "It is my impression that no one really likes the new. We are afraid of it. It is not only as Dostoyevsky put it that 'taking a new step, uttering a new word is what people fear most.' Even in slight things the experience of the new is rarely without some stirring of foreboding.

"Back in 1936 I spent a good part of the year picking peas. I started out in early January, in the Imperial Valley and drifted northward, picking peas as they ripened, until I picked the last peas of the season, in June, around Tracy. Then I shifted all the way to Lake County, where for the first time I was going to pick string beans. And I still remember how hesitant I was that first morning as I was about to address myself to the string bean vines. Would I be able to pick string beans? Even the change from peas to string beans had in it elements of fear.

"In the case of drastic change the uneasiness is of course deeper and more lasting. We can never be really prepared for that which is wholly new. We have to adjust ourselves, and every radical adjustment is a crisis in self-esteem: we undergo a test, we have to prove ourselves. It needs inordinate self-cofidence to face drastic change without inner trembling."[18]

The Christian leader must be conscious of the basic roots of behavior, without overlooking the Christian motivation distinguishing the community of the redeemed. In dealing with group members Jesus did not overlook their basic or learned needs. This can be observed in his dealings with the Twelve. Peter was the recognized spokesman, the man with high prestige. John was particularly sensitive to the Master, Peter, John, and Andrew were often associated with the Lord in unique experiences. Jesus varied his answers in dealing with the Apostles, meeting their specific needs. Encouragement and rebuke were not distributed evenly. Each situation required sensitivity and the specific needs of each member of the apostolic circle were recognized.

A study of the relationship between Jesus and the Twelve and Jesus and the crowd would yield interesting insight into group dynamics. God, who planted these needs for security, approval, and recognition into the human heart, can satisfy them. They are met through a personal relationship with God, but also through the tangible fellowship of believers.

---

[18]Eric Hoffer, *Ordeal of Change* (N.Y., Harper & Row), 1963, p. 3.

10

The Situation

Leadership style is determined by three factors: the personality of the leader, the nature and expectation of the group, and the existential situation.

Under the broad heading "situation" we should consider the prevailing mood of the age, the temper of the times.

It has always been difficult to explain the abundance of leadership talent at certain times in history, over against the extreme penury of the same commodity at other times. Why was the prophetic voice silent from Malachi to John the Baptist? Why were Moses and Joshua followed by the Judges, most of whom hardly deserved the title of leader? Why were Pericles, Sophocles, and Phidias all living in Athens in the fifth century B.C.? What brought the great musicians Beethoven, Mozart, and Haydn together at Vienna? Why were Washington, Jefferson, and Madison contemporaries in Virginia, each one a capable political leader? Why did the same era produce Michelangelo, Raphael, Leonardo da Vinci, and Titian in Italy? Why does our own generation seem to be deficient in leadership?

It may not be possible to furnish a complete answer to these questions, but it is interesting that the same phenomenon can be observed in the history of the kingdom of God. At times there was an abundance of creative and imaginative leadership, followed by periods of great dearth. Anselm of Canterbury (1034-1109), Peter Abelard (1079-1142), Bernard of Clairvaux, Hugo of St. Victor (1096-1141), Peter Lombard (1100-1160) leading to the high point of scholasticism, and Thomas Aquinas (1224-1274) were succeeded by weak epigones. Luther, Calvin, Melanchthon, Zwingli, and other reformers such as Thomas Cranmer, John Knox, and Martin Bucer were only three generations removed from mediocrity.

The ninety-five theses of Luther created an immense sensation, expressing, as they did, what many others felt. The ingredients for explosion were present. The time was ripe, the crucial moment had come. Luther contributed distinctive features to what followed, but it would almost seem that someone else would have given the decisive impulse, had Luther failed to do so.

Regarding the simultaneous emergence of Washington, Jefferson, and Madison, it could perhaps be said that the New World offered few opportunities for the display of leadership and talent, *except* in the public arena. Perhaps the field of politics was the one area of challenge, urging and inviting because of the specific need of that day. There were few temptations to distract talented men from preoccupations with public concerns. The arts did not flourish. Political problems were uppermost in everyone's mind. Similarly, the fact that so much artistic creativity was centered in Florence at one particular point of history may be due to the fact that the artist was held in high esteem. Could the same be true of the great musicians mentioned previously or of the abundance of scientists in our own generation? When theology was held in high esteem, the best thinkers entered into that particular field and excelled. Creative persons can excel in different fields of endeavor and will automatically gravitate to the field which promises maximum outreach and influence. This seems to be a logical inference. Leonardo da Vinci may be an outstanding and perhaps extreme illustration of this fact.

Ehud, Gideon, and Jephthah did not seem eminently fitted for the task of leadership, but perhaps their contemporaries could not esteem better men. There may have been some in the midst of Israel, ready to act fearlessly and with high motivation, but the tribes would have been unable to follow their lofty ideals.

The reformer before his time remains unknown, either eclipsed or martyred. If he obtains influence it will not last because he cannot find support.

The effective leader must take the historic situation into consideration. A democratic style of leadership would have been unthinkable at certain times in history when the autocratic ideal prevailed. Such a style of leadership would hardly be suitable to any one of the popes. Teamwork, characteristic of the scientific approach in the U.S., would have been ill fated in ages of strong individualism.

Before his ascension, Jesus spoke to his diciples of "times and seasons" in the history of the kingdom of God. Similarly, the book of Ecclesiastes reminds us that there is a time for everything and that everything is appropriate in its own time. The author links leadership to specific situations and relates the story of a besieged city wherein a poor, but wise man rose to temporary prominence because "he knew what to do to save the city, and so it was rescued. But afterwards no one thought any more about him" (9:15).

Many a leader may die unknown and fail to find acceptance because the tide of history has not moved in his direction, or because the situation did not provide an opportune moment. Luther was effective where John Hus seemed to have failed. Hus took a position closely akin to the one maintained by Luther a century later. He was burned at the stake—and although this did not end the movement he had initiated, it did not start the Reformation.

When Jesus began preaching the gospel of God, he said: The time is fulfilled (Mk. 1:15). Paul reminds us that the incarnation of the Son of God occurred "when the time had fully come"—but Jesus was rejected by his contemporaries.

Moses assumed that his brothers would understand that God planned to deliver them through him. Israel failed to understand, and rejected his leadership. Moses was compelled to flee to the land of Midian because of his own countrymen. Obviously the time was not ripe. We do not know why Moses expected his countrymen to understand that God would use him to bring freedom to the enslaved nation. Forty years later the mood of history changed and Moses became a recognized leader (Acts 7:23ff).

Aside from such broader historic considerations, the leader must also consider the specific, actual moment, the opportunity. The words of Jesus regarding the "times and seasons" in the kingdom of God have been alluded to. The first word, "times," refers to time from the standpoint of duration or extension, as the German word Zeit*raum*. The word translated "seasons" refers to the joints or articulations in these times, the critical, epoch-making periods foreordained of God, the decisive moments, or the German Zeit*punkt*. It is the latter concept of time which needs additional consideration in relation to leadership. The leader must know the propitious hour, the crucial point, the decisive moment. He must give thoughtful consideration to the specific circumstances and buy up the opportunities. His insight must extend not only to the general mood but also to the specific moment.

Solomon had devised an excellent administrative plan. He divided the land into twelve districts for tax purposes. These geographic districts did not coincide with the ancient tribal boundaries. Solomon undoubtedly hoped to break up the tribal pattern which had played such a large and negative role under Saul and David. Solomon hoped to create a national consciousness, to set an efficient administration in motion, to exercise better tax control and to erect the Temple as a national center of spiritual unity. During his reign his measures prevailed and were successfully implemented. Upon his death the matter of taxes was hotly debated. Rehoboam refused to yield to the demands of the ten tribes and ancient jealousies revived. The Solomonic kingdom broke up and henceforth the nation was divided into the kingdom of Judah and the kingdom of Israel. Solomon's strong personality prevailed over the temper of the times. He saw the opportune moment to implement his reforms and seized it. His successor did not have the necessary wisdom, and, despising the advice of the elders, forfeited the opportunity to become ruler of a united nation.

"It must be recognized that the leader cannot create the conditions which make the rise of a movement possible. He cannot conjure a movement out of the void. There must be eagerness to follow, an intense dissatisfaction with things as they are, before movement and leader can make their appearance. When conditions are not ripe, the potential leader, no matter how gifted, and his holy cause, no matter how potent, remain without a following."[1] The leader emerges as such because he articulates the goals and embodies the ideals which arouse wide following.

The life of Winston Churchill furnishes an excellent illustration. He had to wait for the opportune moment before he could play his leadership role. In the decade of the thirties he was well known but did not have a sufficient following. When disaster shook the country to its foundation, at the most crucial moment, Churchill came into his own. The willingness to wait, the ability to seize the opportune moment and to enter the scene at the crucial point in the course of history—these are part of the necessary ingredients for leadership. It must be recognized that longevity plays a role. If Moses had died at 79 he might only be known as a man who had unsuccessfully tried to liberate his nation and who had fled into exile when he failed. In fact, he might not be known at all. Adenauer only reached the peak at the age of 73, after having been dismissed as mayor of Cologne four years sooner by the British occupation authorities. De Gaulle reached the high point of leadership at the age of 68 when he emerged as the only personality capable of inspiring popular confidence. One must live long enough to be available when the opportune moment finally arrives. This is hardly in the control of any leader, even the best.

The prevailing mood in the United States favors democratic ideals. There are minorities with differing viewpoints and within the broad spectrum of democratic principles, some groups are more conservative and others more liberal, but generally speaking, democratic ideals have permeated American society—though the implementation of these ideals in specific areas be ever so weak. This does not necessarily mean that the democratic style of leadership is the only one prevailing in politics, business, and every other field of endeavor. It does mean, however, that group leadership is of peculiar significance in the United States as over

[1]Eric Hoffer, *The True Believer,* p. 103.

against other countries where dictatorships prevail and authoritarian forms of government are more acceptable. At the same time, it must be remembered that in the U.S. various styles of leadership have been successfully adopted.

The Situation in the United States

It would be erroneous to assume that a Christian leader is automatically committed to a specific style of leadership. Various forms of government have prevailed in the church, ranging from the Episcopalian to the Congregational system, from an authoritarian type of church government to a highly democratic form. In these matters the church often reflects the temper of the times. Quite obviously, the Episcopalian structure of the early centuries was a copy of the Roman system. The fact that every advocate of a specific form of church government refers to the Scripture only enhances the confusion. The Scriptures contain very little information regarding church government, leaving the matter rather flexible. In the light of the changing conditions of the church across history and in different nations this is certainly not accidental.

The Christian leader must consider his own character, the needs of the group, and the specific situation. Almost every style of leadership has advantages and disadvantages, and practically every style of leadership has at one time or other emerged in the church of Jesus Christ. This last statement might come as a surprise. Can a genuine Christian leader ever be autocratic? Jesus condemned tyrannical power and spoke of a different order in the kingdom of God. The autocrat does not serve as Jesus demanded of his followers. Such leadership does not permit the expansion of freedom which is the goal of redemptive, Christian leadership. The autocratic leader enslaves people. He intends to rule and is driven by lust for power.

Ellsworth Toohey, one of the characters in *The Fountainhead,* flatly declares that he shall rule the world. "I intended to rule . . . I shall rule . . . it is only a matter of discovering the lever. If you learn how to rule one single man's soul, you can get the rest of mankind . . . There are many ways (of obtaining control); here's one. Make man feel small. Make him feel guilty. Kill his aspiration and his integrity . . . Kill man's sense of values. Kill his capacity to recognize greatness or to achieve it . . . Enshrine mediocrity . . . Don't let anything remain sacred in a man's soul—and his soul won't be sacred to him . . . Take away from them whatever is dear or important to them. Never let them have what they want. Make them feel that the mere fact of a personal desire is evil . . . Empty man's soul—and the space is yours to fill.[2]

The autocratic leader identifies a problem, selects a solution and simply tells his followers what to do. In his deliberations he may or may not consider the group feeling about this decision and enforce his will by direct or indirect pressure.

The picture of the dictatorial leader is somber because the human heart is dark. This style of leadership could be ideal if the leader were perfect in wisdom and love. The sovereignty of God, the kingship of Christ fall into this unusual category. Some of the great Christian leaders have been autocrats. John Wesley was among them. He "kept an autocratic control."[3] For a time, Wesley himself visited each of the societies to supervise them and to enforce discipline. Not that Wesley was inflexible. When some laymen began preaching, Wesley demurred. His mother admonished him that in so doing he might be thwarting the Holy Spirit. He yielded.

Generally speaking, even the most autocratic leader must consider his followers. Henry VIII was one of the great autocratic leaders, yet even he was careful not to move until he was fairly confident of carrying the bulk of public opinion with him. His real strength lay in his popularity with the majority of the people. Such a leader may well make the decision without consultation, but he senses the temper of the times. Instead of merely announcing his decision he tries to persuade the group members to accept it.

At this point we are moving closer to the democratic style. In the U.S. most leaders—Christian or otherwise—at least pay lip service to democratic principles. This covers a broad range. The

---

[2]Ayn Rand, *op. cit.*, p. 636 ff.
[3]Kenneth Scott Latourette, *A History of Christianity* (N.Y., Harper & Row), 1953, p. 1027.

leader may allow the group members to influence his decision from the very beginning. The problem is presented. Consultation follows. The leader selects the best solution. The leader may go a step further. He may participate in the discussion simply as another member of the group and carry out the group concensus. At this point it may be difficult to determine what are the standards by which to determine if one is cooperating or surrendering. The redemptive leader should be more than a neutral lubricant of other human beings. He should be identified with a challenge and a goal. Should the leader concentrate on personality relationships within the group, or focus primary attention on the goal? Is his task to keep people happy? Is not creativity, which implies change, always resisted? As someone else put it: "If the corporation concentrates on getting people who will process other peoples ideas, where will it get the other people—that is the people with the ideas?"[4]

Under the protective umbrella of democratic ideals it is easy to shirk leadership responsibilities and to "pass the buck." The leader may be tempted to be popular rather than right, to be guided rather than to lead. He may take his cue from opinion polls and be swayed by the crowd, which in many cases amounts to abdication of responsibility. The conflict and tension between responsibility and responsiveness is not easily resolved, but must be attempted by the democratic leader. On the one hand he should allow group participation to increase commitment and motivation; on the other hand he is asked to be efficient, which often necessitates solo decisions to save time.

Democratic leadership may sink to the level of colorless mediocrity. Only the average is right, good, and fair. It would be absurd to deprecate superior vitality on the ground that only average health is fair and normal. Does a genuine leader search concensus or mold concensus? Martin Luther King Jr. said on one occasion: "If every Negro in the United States turns to violence, I will choose to be that one lone voice preaching that this is the wrong way." He then commented: "Maybe this sounded like arrogance. But it was not intended that way. It was simply

[4]William H. White, Jr., *op. cit.*, p. 150.

my way of saying that I would rather be a man of *conviction* than a man of conformity. Occasionally in life one develops a conviction so precious and meaningful that he will stand on it till the end. This is what I have found in nonviolence."[5]

An essay in *Time* spells it out: "A President has to establish moral authority based on public trust. Indeed, the whole art of governing a democracy lies in mustering popular consent on a vast scale. A President must have convictions, a vision of where the nation should travel; he must summon the national mood and push it in the right direction. If he fails to give his people a sense of participation in crucial decisions, his politics may be doomed from the start. 'A President' says political scientist James MacGregor Burns, 'must be both preacher and politician.' "

It remains true that "Those (Presidents) who grow acquire a sense of history, a feeling that the right moment has come for the right innovation—and the confidence to forge ahead when the people are not quite ready."[6]

That which is to be in the future but cannot be realized today must be a flaming vision for the leader.

It is hardly necessary to illustrate the large number of Christian leaders, especially in the last hundred years, who have adopted a democratic style of leadership, be it at one or the other end of the broad spectrum.

Because theological convictions come into play and because of a strong assurance of the will of God, the partisan style of leadership is often adopted—although probably under the guise of democratic principles. That this is at the root of many divisions in the church is self-evident. That many a great work has been pioneered by a leader with a narrow focus cannot be contested.

Interestingly enough, the Bible contains special warnings against the party-spirit. "Do nothing from selfishness" (Phil. 2:3 RSV) or "strife" (AV). Originally, the Greek word describes someone working for hire, a hireling, a partisan who does not disdain the low arts of intrigue. Everything is done in a mercenary spirit.

---

[5]Martin Luther King, Jr., *Where Do We Go From Here: Chaos or Community?* (N.Y., Harper & Row), 1967, pp. 63–64.
[6]*Time,* July 26, 1968.

This stands in perfect juxtaposition with the word "conceit" which follows. What are these two tempers condemned by the apostle? The first is the spirit which unduly exalts the party and the second the spirit which unduly exalts self. The two are not unallied, and their objects are different. The Apostle treats them together, but treats them as distinct. They are two species of the genus.

The first word denotes the temper, habit, principal action of the hireling, the hired partisan. The word designates the party spirit generally. In some form or other, gain to self is achieved through the triumph of the party. Though the direct object is not self, yet ultimately this spirit may be traced to self. The conceit which is condemned by Paul is the inflated estimate of one's own ability, one's own reputation, one's own position and importance. The former is the more insidious and therefore the more dangerous vice of the two, because conceit carries its own condemnation on its face. But the spirit of partisanship has a specious side. It is even possible to proclaim Christ out of partisanship (Phil. 1:17) from base and corrupt motives. In this case the triumph of the party stands first and the triumph of the Gospel holds only a subordinate place. The party spirit masks itself, disguises its true character. Its object may be something eminently good and true in itself. It may display its activity in the dissemination of the truth or in the defense of the church of God. But it arrogates to itself the respect and honor which belongs to the object of its pursuit.

Since we live in an age of conflict and since the truth by which we live is bitterly and relentlessly attacked, defense becomes a necessity. Defense implies organization. Men must be gathered together; they must have a rallying point. They must be taught to act in concert. Yet this banding together in the face of an opponent tends to become the very seed of party spirit. This party spirit may well be the last infirmity of the religious man, the zealous follower of Christ, follower at least (at however great a distance) in his zeal and self-devotion; but not follower in his wide sympathy, not follower in his large charity, not follower in his concessive indulgent moderation which is the direct negation of partisan zeal. The antidote is found in the following words of Paul: "But in humility count others better than yourselves" (Phil. 2:3).

As to situational leadership, it has been suggested that a spontaneous, unrehearsed leader emerges in a crisis and elicits spontaneous response. The leader clarifies and suggests. He is the first among equals, a member of the group. His action flows from interpersonal and reciprocal relationship of group members as they are controlled and guided by the purposes and objectives of the group. Given a different situation, the leadership might change. Actually, there is some evidence to suggest that leadership remains constant, regardless of the group situation. Regardless of the situation of the Twelve, the primary group was always composed of Peter, John, and Andrew. Peter was the leader in all situations. Most of the members in the apostolic group never emerged as group leaders. Similarly, the men surrounding Paul recognized in him a leader whose position did not vary with the situation.

Many other factors come into play where the style of leadership is concerned. The best style of leadership is the one best suited to accomplish the task. The potential leader must know something about his own personality. What is his own style? He must analyze the group. Are the members mature and experienced enough to assume responsibility? Do they understand the goals and expect to share in the decision-making process? How has the group performed in the past? The situation must be diagnosed. Does the style meet the expectation of the group? What are the conditions facilitating or complicating the task? The leadership style to be adopted is determined by all these factors, but the basic Christian motivation is the key factor.

At the antipode of the Christian concept of leadership stands the following description of a hero: "His vision, his strength, his courage came from his own spirit. A man's spirit, however, is his self . . . It is the whole secret of his power—that he was self-sufficient, self-motivated, self-generated. The leader is a first cause, a fount of energy, a life force, a Prime Mover. He served nothing and no one. He lived for himself. And only by living for himself was he able to achieve the things which are the glory of mankind. Such is the nature of achievement."[7]

In reality, the vision, strength, and courage of the Christian leader come from God. He serves others—redemptively. This last element is supremely important. It is possible to serve people in order to enslave them or to maintain them in a state of dependency, never achieving freedom. The advisors of King Rehoboam suggested he yield to the demands of the people; serve them—and they will serve you (I Kgs. 12:7).

The touchstone of redemptive service is the relation between the leader and the one next in line. "In the case of a leader, perhaps the hardest thing is to help those who stand immediately next—those who hold the trying position of second in command, or who are near enough to the front to be constantly impressed by the fact that they fall short of being at the front. The temptation to treat them as possible rivals and to depreciate their gifts instead of magnifying them is constant to everyone but a truly great man. The Christian leader with redemptive purposes will teach and train (= serve) the "next in line." He will develop his potential, allow the free play of his personality, liberate him rather than enslave or dominate him for selfish purposes. This does not mean that he relinquishes control or allows men to use him, any more than Jesus permitted men to take advantage of him.

This relationship to the second in command is also discussed in *Moby Dick:* "Now, as you well know, it is not seldom the case in this conventional world of ours—watery or otherwise, that when a person placed in command over his fellow-men finds one of them to be very significantly his superior in general pride of manhood, straightway against that man he conceives an unconquerable dislike and bitterness; and if he have a chance he will pull down and pulverize that subaltern's tower, and make a little heap of dust of it."[8]

Is this what happened to the French Premier Pompidou in May, 1968? Was he fired by General DeGaulle because the Premier had become too popular? Wilhelm II fired Bismarck in 1890.

[7]Ayn Rand, *op. cit.,* p. 680.
[8]*Idem.,* pp. 260–261.

DeGaulle dismissed Michel Debre after the latter had presided over the unpleasant Algerian affair. Later DeGaulle fired Pompidou, who kept the government running during the May riots in 1968. Pompidou masterminded the campaign which brought DeGaulle back into power. His reward was to be dismissed. His success became a threat to DeGaulle. Willful and arbitrary, DeGaulle acted in true autocratic fashion, retaining a firm grip on the levers of power. The attitude of the Christian leader becomes clear by contrast. Style is an important element, but not the key factor—motivation is the essential one. The Christian motivation also becomes the foundation for leadership training.

Leadership in the Family

It is relatively easy to think of leadership in the context of a large corporation—and to ignore the concept in the restricted sphere of the family. But the principles of Christian leadership should work in the smallest social unit as well as on a national scale.

Leadership in the family covers only one particular aspect of family relationships; therefore the emphasis of these pages is necessarily one-sided. According to the Scriptures the husband should be the leader of the family. This creates a number of difficulties. It makes the role of the wife exceedingly difficult if she is superior to her husband in talent or capacity. In other spheres a change of leadership is possible, but not in the family. Therefore, extraordinary love and patience are needed, but the biblical principle remains firm.

The authority of the husband is based on love and received on a religious basis. This is made explicit by Paul in a number of biblical passages. He writes "I want you to understand that the head of every man is Christ, the head of a woman is her husband, and the head of Christ is God" (I Cor. 11:3). The Christian order is that the man is the head of the woman, Christ is the head of man, God is the head of Christ. Authority springs from union, be it the union of marriage between husband and wife, the union of faith between Christ and man, the union of essence between Christ and God. The nature of these unions is altogether different, and so is the nature of the authority. Man is not the head of the woman in the same sense as Christ is the head of man. There is a tremendous difference between the union of faith between God and man and the union of marriage. The preeminence which Paul advocates is determined by the context. Regardless of the sphere wherein the authority is exercised, it is essential that it be based on a community of life, on participation, on fellowship. The authority of Christ is founded on his redemptive work and the purpose of the headship of Christ is the growth and development of the body. The same holds true in family relationships. The authority has union for its ground and redemption for its object. Christ is the head, not to enslave, but to set free through redemption and the same idea should prevail in the small circle of the family.

In respect of salvation there is no difference between man and wife because in Christ there is neither male nor female (Gal. 3:28). But the social distinctions remain. Paul re-emphasizes the same thought when he writes to the Ephesians: Wives, be subject to your husbands, as to the Lord (5:22). The submission of the wife to the leadership of the husband is treated as a religious obligation expressed in the words "as to the Lord." The word "as" does not imply similarity—the submission is not unconditional even as to Jesus Christ—but it is rendered as part of the obedience *to* Jesus Christ. Subjection does not imply inferiority. Paul reminds both husband and wives of their duties, not of their rights.

It is really very simple. In the family there must be leadership and the responsibility of that leadership belongs to the husband. Upon him Paul imposes an even greater obligation when he writes: Husbands, love your wives, as Christ loved the church and gave himself up for her. Once again the redemptive concept of leadership is stressed. Christ gave himself in order to santify the church, that he might present her in splendor, holy and without blemish. The willing subjection of the wife is her response to the redemptive leadership of the husband. It is a subjection which is not conditioned by the demands of external law but carried out in the energy of love. The demands of law are exceeded, the highest law of love and redemption prevails, true leadership is exercised and harmony is achieved.

The expression "and a little child shall lead them" (Isa. 11:6) reflects a highly poetic description of peace and security, when animals of all descriptions live together harmoniously and when even those who are defenseless can live in security. When the natural ferocity of animals is tamed and they can be led by a little child, the messianic age will have dawned. Until that day, the principles of leadership just outlined apply also in relation to children. It is a great temptation for parents to enslave their children, to force them into conformity with the parental image. Little scope is left for self-expression and for the development of the child's individuality. Such an attitude is not redemptive, does not lead to maturity or freedom. At the same time it must be stressed, especially in our day, that discipline is part of the maturing process and when applied wisely does not hinder individual development.

Fathers, notice the emphasis, are admonished not to provoke their children to anger (Eph. 6:4). Parental leadership is not a reign of terror. Punishment is not administered to gratify ill humor. Unnecessary irritation through unreasonable treatment is not redemptive. Paul also stresses a more positive aspect: Bring up children in the discipline and instruction of the Lord. The most prominent element of education is discipline. The purpose of this discipline must be kept in view. The primary concern of parents is to lead their children to a knowledge of God, that they may serve the counsel of God in their own generation.

As might be expected, obedience is the key word addressed to children. To submit to restraints which are acknowledged to be expedient and reasonable is a poor test of obedience. To submit where restraints seem unnecessary is more difficult. If it is the duty of parents not to be capricious or unreasonable, it is the duty of children to recall that there can be no obedience without authority. How this authority should be exercised is the key problem. It should not be to the point of provoking anger but with the redemptive concept that the loyalty of children to Christ is far more important than anything else. The style of leadership which is adopted could, within certain limits, vary from child to child. The personality of each child has to be taken into consideration. But regardless of the specific situation, leadership should never be abdicated and the application of Christian principles of leadership, which have already been spelled out, should yield optimum effectiveness.

11

Can Leaders Be Trained?

Is leadership training possible? As previously stated, it was assumed for centuries that leadership was inherited. Leaders were born—not made. Leadership was a monopoly of the aristocracy. With the overthrow of feudal nobility and the rise of democracy, a new leadership concept was born. It appeared that leadership can be learned. The focus shifted to the personality of the leader.

Recently, the "great man" theory was developed. It was assumed that certain innate characteristics and qualities equip the leader for his role. He would be a man of distinctive stamp, predestined by his unusual capacity to become a leader, controlling events and molding situations.

Pragmatically speaking, the ability of the leader must meet specific needs of the group and fit the existential situation. As more attention was paid to this aspect of the problem, the center of gravity shifted from the person of the leader to the function of the group. Leadership was now seen as a group property and as a function of the group structure. The significance of the leader is still recognized, but largely because he is seen as the dynamic focus of the group.

Finally, it has been suggested that leadership is situational. It is argued that a leader may be ineffective in situations where his abilities are not useful. Since personality traits are stable or fixed, whereas group goals and purposes are variable, it has been deduced that leadership must be fluid and move from one member of the group to another, depending on the situation.

We are then face to face with three basic concepts of leadership: the center of gravity is either in the leader, in the group, or in the situation.

Today, relatively few specialists subscribe to the "great man" theory of leadership. In a mood of pessimism and despair man would rather trace events to fatal forces and demonic influences, than to human initiative. As long as a positive, hopeful outlook prevailed, historians were glad to attribute foresight and genius to the great leaders of mankind. Failure produced a reversal. Nobody wanted to be responsible for the holocaust produced by two world wars, or for nuclear extinction. All has become impersonal, and responsibility has shifted from men and leaders to situations beyond our control. Convenient—but not convincing! It is unrealistic not to recognize that in any given group some persons are better equipped, by virtue of their characteristics, to serve as leaders. All desirable leadership attributes are not equally capable of self-cultivation or development. Some attributes are innate. Obviously, all the necessary qualities do not appear in every leader to the same extent, regardless of careful training. It does remain true that leadership can be learned and developed . . . at least to some extent. Some persons have acquired qualities of personality without conscious effort which equip them in a unique way for leadership. Other qualities can be learned and potential ones can be developed.

It is an "unarguable fact that most human beings go through their lives only partially aware of the full range of their abilities."[1] Perhaps this is due to a confusion between genius and talent. Genius, a word derived from the Latin meaning literally, "the begetter," refers to creative ability demonstrated by actual achievement. It may be a combination of intellect and zeal. Since genius runs in families—and one of the most outstanding illustrations is the family of Johann Sebastian Bach—it has been related to nature. Other studies stress nurture. The truth is undoubtedly in the middle. Genius is not exclusively in the nature of an inheritance. John Bunyan's father was a poor tinker. Shakespeare, Keats, and

[1]John W. Gardner, *Self Renewal,* p. 10.

Lincoln were born in mediocre families. It is true that a larger percentage of superior offspring arise from distinguished parents, but this could be related to the sociological factors involved. If aptitude is inherited, the potential ability often depends on the environment for development. The relationship to God—the greatest environmental factor—is critical. But genius must not be confused with general leadership or talent.

Genius is a revelation of a man's creative nature, of his calling to creativity. It is incompatible with a safe-and-sound worldly attitude. Genius cannot yield to the demands of the world and life tends to be one of sacrificial heroism. The genius is usually in tragic disharmony with the world.

Talent is more functional and adaptable to the demands of contemporary culture. Talent is moderate. Genius is measureless. The nature of genius is revolutionary. Talent acts in the midst of culture with its arts and sciences. Genius acts in ends and beginnings and knows no bounds. Talent is obedience; genius is daring.[2]

In the parable of Jesus, the man who had received one talent was tempted not to use it. The men more richly endowed were conscious of their abilities and used them. "There are qualities genetically and socially inherited that incline some persons toward leadership more than others . . . Then there are qualities to be acquired through process of learning and experience."[3]

Peter the Great (1772-1825), Emperor of Russia, believed in leadership training. The secret of his extraordinary success lay in the fact that he organized an informal but highly effective training system for turning out young men who would serve his revolutionary purposes. Peter the Great recognized the requirements of the Russian nation and his obligation as its ruler. It would have simplified his task had he placed intelligent foreigners at the head of every department of State, allowing them gradually to train up a native bureaucracy. But he was determined that at whatever cost, hardship, or inconvenience, Russia should be ruled by Russians, not by foreigners. Before his death every important place in the empire was in the hands of capable Russians of his own training. Even in his most seething reforms he never lost sight of the idio-

[2]Cf. Nicolas Berdyaev, *op. cit.*, pp. 162–163.
[3]Gaines S. Dobbins, *Learning to Lead* (Nashville, Tenn., Broadman Press), 1968, p. 14.

syncracies of his nation. He never destroyed anything which he was not able to replace with something better. One can hardly endorse his personality, marked by violent passions and cyclonic rage. His hatred rarely stopped short of extermination; his banquets were orgies and his pastimes convulsions. Nevertheless, and in spite of his unstable personality, he had extraordinary talent which made his work possible and his training system highly effective.

The church of Jesus Christ is facing a similar challenge in many countries of the world where younger churches are at work. It is absolutely imperative to find training systems which will enable these churches to function in an era characterized by nationalism. It is the avowed aim of Christian mission societies to bring a strong national church into being. Such a church cannot emerge without capable leadership. Therefore, as Christians, we must believe in the possibility of leadership training and devise methods whereby this goal can be achieved.

It might be safe to assume that of all the vocations of life the one that cannot be trained for is the prophetic vocation. The prophet is a man responding to the call of God. How can he be trained? It would seem that no amount of training could prepare a man to play the role of a prophet.

It is all the more interesting to consider the "schools of the prophets" established and headed by Samuel (I Sam. 19:19-20). In the days of Elijah and Elisha, schools were maintained at Gilgal, Bethel and other cities (II Kgs. 2:1; 3:4,38; 6:1). Into these schools the promising students were gathered and trained for the office which they were destined to fill. As a result, from the days of Solomon to the very last days of the kingdom of Judah, there always was an adequate supply of men to fill the ranks of official prophets. They were developed, trained, and educated in the prophetic schools. Spiritual gifts can be developed.

By way of contrast it is important to notice that before the call of Samuel, who established such schools, the prophetic word was rare in Israel and prophecy was not widespread. These training schools undoubtedly played a significant role and resulted in the uninterrupted succession of prophets in the kingdom of Judah across the centuries.

Jesus spent a major portion of his time with the disciples with the distinct purpose to train the Twelve. Toward the end of his life he said: I have told these men all about you . . . For I have passed on to them the commands you gave me; and they took them and know of a certainty that I came down to earth from you, and they believe you sent me (Jn. 17:6,8).

According to the Gospel of Mark, at three distinct moments Jesus isolated himself with the Twelve for more specific indoctrination and training. Leadership training is part of the biblical pattern. Moses and Joshua, Elijah and Elisha, Jesus, and the Twelve, Paul and Timothy—these are only a few of the most outstanding examples.

Perhaps there is an unconscious reluctance to train leaders, because training makes men knowledgeable. They soon assess their superiors and may become critical. Redemptive Christian leadership is not influenced by such considerations. Training is always opposed both to the dictatorial and the paternalistic style of leadership. Could it be that too many in the church of God are either dictatorial or paternalistic—whether here or abroad—and for this reason the church has been slow in training capable national leaders?

It goes without saying that it is precisely in the area of leadership training that the redemptive viewpoint of Christian leadership plays a significant role. Are leaders scarce beoause our thinking is not redemptive, because opportunity is not furnished, because training is not available? Where is the bottleneck?

Many people would certainly like to become leaders and among them some should have the required capacities. Is the recruiting system inadequate? Is selection a problem? By what mechanism do we determine who should be trained for leadership? How do we discover the best people with the greatest potential? Does a criterion have an oppressive effect upon the creative person? At this point, spiritual discernment becomes paramount because the pursuit of excellence cannot simply be based on mechanical rules of conduct or upon tests or achievement. It is for this very reason that Jesus spent a night in prayer before choosing the Twelve. We do not know what dictated the choice of these men, but his expectation was largely justified by the results.

Leadership training can flourish only in a positive atmosphere.

Opportunities for maturing latent leadership must be developed. The existence of such opportunities implies a willingness to share the leadership role. Moses rejoiced when the Spirit of God fell upon the seventy elders of Israel. Even Eldad and Medad, two elders who remained in the camp, received a special measure of the Spirit of God and began to prophesy. When Moses and Joshua received word about this, Joshua commanded: My lord Moses, forbid them. But Moses answered: Are you jealous for my sake? Would that all the Lord's people were prophets, that the Lord would put his Spirit on them (Num. 11). There was no leadership monopoly, no jealousy, no exclusiveness. Seventy people received the opportunity to share the leadership role.

Moses deliberately trained Joshua. The latter had grown up as a slave in the brick fields of Egypt. Liberated through the exodus, Joshua was found at the side of Moses in the battle against the Amalekites. He was the constant companion of the great leader, even walking up the slopes of Mt. Sinai to receive the Ten Commandments. Joshua was one of the twelve chiefs to explore the land of Canaan. Upon the death of Moses, Joshua became the undisputed leader of Israel. In about six years he conquered the land of Canaan. He died at the age of 110, the last survivor of a famous generation.

Moses had carefully trained Joshua as his successor—but he did not make the choice in an autocratic fashion. When this great leader was informed that he should be gathered to his ancestors, he put away all selfish thoughts and merely prayed that God would appoint a man over Israel to lead them, so that the congregation would not be as sheep without a shepherd (Num. 27:18). At that point God confirmed the choice Moses had made and Joshua was commissioned leader in the sight of the nation. For forty years Moses and Joshua labored together and Moses was willing to share the responsibilities of leadership with Joshua and to train him through several decades.

Joshua became the leader of Israel at the age of 85 and remained at the helm for 25 years. Sometimes longevity may be a decisive factor. Had John Wesley died at age 35, he would not have been remembered. Contemporaries might have described him as a methodical, hard-working, but pedantic and legalistic man.

At the most, one might have said that he was sincere but a failure as a missionary.

Kant published his first great work at the age of 58. If he had died at age 48 he might be relatively unknown. The most striking illustrations in our day are certainly Churchill, Adenauer, and De Gaulle. Since the average length of life in many countries is as much as one-third shorter than in the U.S., the urgency of the early leadership training is highlighted!

An additional reason for early leadership training is the flexibility of youth. Mature people learn far less than young people because age has made them rigid and they are not willing to take risks, to innovate. Learning is a risky business because it results in change and an alteration in the status quo might spell failure. It is safer not to change, i.e. not to learn. Concentrate training efforts on youth! Paul was always surrounded by younger men, whom he trained as future leaders of the church. Paul and Barnabas used John as an assistant. Later Barnabas continued John Mark's training and Paul also kept in touch with him. The Apostle of the Gentiles also trained Silas and Timothy, travelled with Priscilla and Aquila, was surrounded by Sopater, Aristarchus, Secundus, Gaius, Tychicus, and Trophimus. Luke was another disciple and the list is far from complete (Acts 13:5; 15:40; 18:18; 19:22; 20:4, etc.).

Was this training program perhaps largely responsible for the rapid expansion of the early church, which seemingly never lacked leadership? Paul might have pleaded that the call to the apostleship was unique, but he did not hesitate to delegate authority and to invest the next generation with the leadership role. He gladly recognized the God-given potential of those surrounding him and furnished opportunities for exercising leadership roles. If a missionary does not believe in the potential leadership ability of the national with whom he works, he will neither discover nor develop leaders.

William Carey, the great pioneer of modern missions, long before he had gone to any mission field, wrote regarding missionary work: "It might likewise be of importance, if God should bless their labors, for them to encourage any appearances of gifts among the people of their charge; if such should be raised up, many advantages would be derived from their knowledge of the language, and customs of their countrymen; and their change of conduct would give great weight to their ministrations."[4]

This missionary statesman foresaw that God could raise up national leaders and he expressed his basic willingness to share the leadership role with them. An opportunity for encouraging inherent talent to emerge must be furnished. Specific aptitudes may be inherited, but the concrete actualization of abilities is conditioned by environment, by the spiritual, social, and intellectual climate. The potential leader must be given, along with a basic confidence in the trainee, a certain ease or freedom.

In summary, leadership simply cannot be developed unless the right conditions prevail. In the light of the worldwide mission of the church and because a great deal of activity is centered in underdeveloped countries, it may be of particular importance to stress the role of ease in leadership training. The potential leader cannot be confined to menial tasks. There must be a certain freedom or ease. It is impossible to become a leader while living under exhausting circumstances.

The man who lives on the borderline of starvation, engaged in a desperate struggle for survival, can hardly be expected to emerge as a leader. His goals must all be concrete and immediate. There is no time for creativity or for long-range planning. The all-absorbing problem is one of hunger, cold, and survival. "Where people toil from sunrise to sunset for a bare living, they nurse no grievances and dream no dreams. One of the reasons for the unrebelliousness of the masses in China is the inordinate effort required there to scrape together the means of the scantiest subsistence. The intensified struggle for existence is a static rather than a dynamic influence."[5]

Similarly John W. Gardner writes: "Poverty doesn't always bring high motivation; some of the most impoverished populations in the world are the most lethargic. And prosperity doesn't always dampen motivation; indeed, a prosperous society—by virtue of its capacity to extend the range of individual opportunity—

[4]William Carey, *An Enquiry* (London, Kingsgate Press), 1961, p. 76
[5]Eric Hoffer, *op. cit.*, pp. 32–33.

may release energies which would otherwise have lain dormant. Certain kinds of creativity require a reasonable measure of abundance. People under severe deprivation are not free to experiment and to try new ways of doing things. In all creative achievement there is a certain recklessness or gambling quality that is often suppressed in a society close to the margin of survival."[6]

It has been suggested that our best ideas come to us in playful moments. "Archimedes' bathtub and Newton's apple suggest that momentous trains of thought may have their inception in idle musing. The original insight is most likely to come when elements stored in different compartments of the mind drift into the open, jostle one another, and now and then coalesce to form new combinations. It is doubtful whether a mind that is pinned down and cannot drift elsewhere is capable of formulating new questions. It is true that the working of our ideas and insights requires persistent hard thinking, and the inspiration necessary for such a task is probably a by-product of single-minded application. But the sudden illumination and the flash of discovery are not likely to materialize under pressure."[7]

Unfortunately, much of our culture is geared to the immediate, to activism. Success is measured in terms of statistics. The concept of creative leisure is absent. Ultimately, creative thinking in an atmosphere of leisure will probably result in something practical and utilitarian—but this utilitarian goal should not be preeminent in the early stages.

It is not accidental that Moses, who became the first great leader of Israel, had not experienced the degrading life of a slave like all the other Hebrews. The one great leader had been brought up in comparative ease.

Up to a point, the trainee must be delivered from a hand-to-mouth existence for his thinking to rise beyond the immediate, to transcend the daily struggle for survival. Not that handicaps cannot be overcome, but it is possible for the challenge to exceed the capability to the point of arresting fruitful development. Many great leaders have overcome significant obstacles. Handicapped

---

[6]John Gardner, *op. cit.*, p. 19.

[7]Eric Hoffer, *The Ordeal of Change* (N.Y., Harper & Row), 1963, pp. 90–91.

people have left their mark upon the world—both for good and ill. But roadblocks do not automatically produce leaders.

Poverty does not necessarily generate high motivation. Some of the most impoverished people in the world are the most lethargic. Toynbee mentions the arrested civilization of the Eskimos, who were unable to cope with their geographic challenge. People under severe deprivation are not really free to experiment and to try new ways. And yet in all creative achievement there is a certain recklessness, a gambling quality which a society living close to the margin of survival simply cannot afford. To move away from the traditional patterns of life involves a great deal of risk. It is impossible and unrealistic to assume that people living on the border line of starvation would be willing to gamble and to expose themselves to the risk of failure.

It should not be assumed that all difficulties must be moved out of the way of a potential leader. Many people have achieved brilliant leadership in spite of obstacles. Louis Braille accidentally lost the sight of one eye at the age of three and later lost the other eye because of sympathetic inflammation. He developed the Braille system. Demosthenes suffered from a speech impediment but became one of the greatest orators of Greece. Beethoven composed his greatest music while deaf. John Milton was a blind poet. Theodore Roosevelt began life as a sickly child. It has even been suggested that it is not what happens to us that counts, but how we deal with it. Abraham Lincoln grew up in dire poverty and enjoyed less than one year of formal schooling. Lincoln knew defeat in his very first bid for public office. Later he gave the following advice to a young student: "If you are resolutely determined to make a lawyer of yourself, the thing is more than half done already. Always bear in mind that your own resolution to succeed is more important than any other one thing."

It may be that regardless of circumstances the exceptional leader will emerge, but how much potential leadership ability is lost because of insurmountable obstacles will never be known.

Training Program

For an effective leadership training program three decisive steps are necessary:

1. A conscious plan to develop leaders
2. An inventory of leadership positions
3. An inventory of potential leaders

1. *A conscious plan to develop leaders:* It is essential for any organization, or for any leader, to give deliberate and conscious thought to the training of other leaders. This will not happen spontaneously and should not occur haphazardly. It must be a significant and deliberate step. At the same time, it is very important for potential leaders to know that thought is given to leadership development. The organization must recognize its own vital need for innovation. The future leader must see that leadership activity is encouraged, not stifled. The general atmosphere, the framework of expectation, becomes extremely significant. There is a climate for success and a climate for failure. When the organization demands strict conformity and uniformity, when the pressure is such that all personal initiative is frowned upon, when creativity is smothered and uniformity extends even to areas that are non-relevant, then the atmosphere is one of negativism and failure.

When communication is deficient and secrecy becomes a weapon, then younger men feel that they are not "in" and tend to move "out."

When failures and errors are not allowed, and there is no room for mistakes, then risks will not be taken and the creative personality, the innovator, will not use his full capacity. When leisure is reduced to a minimum, creativity is inhibited. Unremitting pressure will be a roadblock to the development of the leadership personality.

2. *An inventory of leadership positions:* It is essential to make an audit, so to speak, of the tasks for which leadership is required. This presupposes that the organization has a long-range plan—flexible perhaps. Good strategy requires an organization chart and people who are deliberately trained to meet specific needs.

Once a potential leader has been identified, a process of training must be initiated. Learning is essentially an internal process. It has been suggested that learning occurs whenever someone experiences a problem or recognizes a gap between the actual and the ideal and then draws on whatever resources are available to acquire the learning necessary to solve the problem or to close the gap. Such resources can be formal or informal, consist of courses or literature, the classroom or experience. Learning involves three factors:

A receiving and responding system

Situations of stimulation

Human association and guidance[8]

Sometimes the entire process of learning has been reduced to two component elements: contact and withdrawal. It is interesting to study both aspects in the life of Christ and in his training of the Apostles.

Learning is efficient only when the goals have been clarified. The trainee has to know specifically what needs to be learned in order to enter into this activity purposefully. His own goals, freely chosen, have to coincide with the goals of the organization.

Learning should result in a change of behavior—and change tends to be resisted. This is one of the key obstacles to learning. It is easier when a person is dissatisfied with his present performance and aspires to improvement. Learning is a difficult and time-consuming process.

3. *An inventory of potential leaders:* This should be based on personal contacts and interviews. Perhaps the choice of future leaders is as difficult as the training. Selection can be based partially on scholastic aptitude tests and achievement tests. Non-academic talents are also essential, such as motives, values, attitudes, judgment and character. The author of Ecclesiastes states: Finishing is better than starting! Patience is better than pride! (7:8). This text is particularly appropriate to leaders. There is no reliable way of measuring such characteristics. Intellect or talent are not the sole keys to a leadership position. There are additional requirements, and paramount among them is a commitment to Jesus Christ and to the redemptive concept of service.

Since tests have only limited value, personal interviews are desirable. The dialogue should at least cover the following:

---

[8]Gaines S. Dobbins, *op cit.*, p. 17.

Sensitivity, the ability to see something to which the average person is blind;

The capacity to stretch perceptual powers;

Flexibility, the ability to adjust quickly to new developments;

Openness, a willingness to abandon old ways and to move beyond the obvious boundaries of the problem. The courage to establish norms;

The ability to abstract, breaking down problems into component parts and combining various elements to form a new whole.

Perhaps more than anything else, motivation is a key factor. The potential leader must have drive, a restless urge, a desire to explore the unknown and the stamina to persevere. Desire, ambition to lead is imperative—if understood in a Christian context. Christian perseverance is not simply bearing things. It is victorious endurance, virile constancy, brave and courageous acceptance of everything life brings, transforming the worst obstacles into stepping-stones. It is the triumphant ability to pass the breaking point without breaking, to greet the unseen with cheer, to hope against hope.

The intellectual qualities can be determined through oral and written examination and an evaluation of the educational record. Technical fitness is discovered by reviewing previous experience. Personal qualities should come to light through interviews. A climate conductive to leadership training demands leadership models.

We emulate a person whom we respect and admire. A boy projects himself into the behavior of his father or teacher. Paul, fully aware of this tendency wrote: Pattern your lives after mine (Phil. 3:17 cf. II Thess. 3:9). Timothy was admonished by Paul to be the ideal of his young disciples (I Tim. 4:12). The pattern is Jesus Christ, who washed the feet of the disciples and said: I have given you an example to follow; do as I have done to you (Jn. 13:15). A slavish imitation of the act is easy but pointless. To serve even as Jesus served, to act in the spirit of humility, is the real issue. He humbled himself to serve and to save. It is this redemptive service which becomes the all-important model for potential leaders.

Group discussions create a climate of creative expectation. Problem-solving clinics can be useful to discover potential leaders. The word "clinic" originally "connoted the instructions given by the physician to the patient at the bedside. Then a gathering of medical specialists studied the patient's symptoms and, after joint consultation, prescribed."[9] The idea of bringing together a group of specialists to discuss different aspects of the problem as it is related to the actual situation is a helpful technique. Similarly, a workshop places leaders in actual situations where, aside from discussion, work is accomplished. A problem has arisen; an answer is needed. Resources are evaluated, goals are clarified, and action is taken.

Small group discussions also stimulate. They should be guided, not dominated, generating light, not heat. Ideas must be freely expressed and all viewpoints must be thoroughly respected.

The right atmosphere for leadership training includes a willingness to share responsibility, to assign specific projects. The one who hopes to become a leader will want to develop leadership qualities. Since the leader should first be a disciple, there must be a willing spirit to carry out orders in a cheerful manner. In other words, the potential leader will be glad to place himself in a training position and to assume minor responsibilities. He needs the experience of the humdrum, the routine, to understand the situation of the people he will supervise later.

According to the Scriptures, the hand of the diligent shall rule, or in a modern paraphrase, "Work hard and become a leader" (Prov. 12:24). The leader is often described as a man who is so completely involved in his work that he cannot distinguish it from the rest of his life—and he is happy that he cannot. Even while the work is completed step by step, the trainee will use his imagination to improve the work and to anticipate the next task. The trainee needs goal-orientation. Training progresses rapidly when the potential leader knows what he is being trained for. He can only be poorly motivated if he does not see the total picture, the ultimate goals.

[9] *Idem.*, p. 24.

It is relatively easy to obtain knowledge on the topic of leadership. It is far more difficult to acquire insight and understanding. Paul's prayer for the Philippians was that they might be more sensitive, more discerning. They needed the ability to apply information and principles to specific situations; to use knowledge obtained in one situation to solve problems in another setting. To define the problem, to analyze the data, to determine the nature and the cause of the problem, to project solutions and to explore alternate solutions, to test the effect of possible answers —these are some of the significant ingredients of leadership.

Sensitivity moves into the realm of the emotions, and feelings are difficult to learn. They are hardly subject to examination or tests. The only way to change an old attitude is to displace it by a new one. This is most encouraging from the Christian perspective since a new power, a new controlling element, is part of the new life.

At this point feedback becomes important and the ability to accept criticism is essential. Paul's prayer for the Philippians is appropriate for every leader and everyone who aspires to leadership: And it is my prayer that your love may abound more and more, with knowledge and discernment, so that you may approve what is excellent, and may be pure and blameless for the day of Christ, filled with the fruits of righteousness which come through Jesus Christ, to the glory and praise of God (Phil. 1:9-11).

Conclusion

Leadership is exercised on many different levels, but the key always remains the leader himself. It is a sad situation when an age is devoid of heroes. It is a somber era when great men are lacking. When it is assumed that fatality rules, that the individual is meaningless, when heroes are lacking, and when homogeneity is more important than excellence, then mediocrity results. When individualism is condemned because it implies dissent, which might lead to conflict; when the greatest industry is to produce conformity, then leadership declines and decay sets in.

Ideas, creativity, courage are indispensable. They are rarely produced by committees. Everything significant begins with an individual. No book stresses this more than the Scripture, where the emphasis falls on individual redemption and the value of one human being.

It goes without saying that everyone must operate within limits. History cannot be propelled into directions for which the environment is not prepared. But it is precisely the redemptive leader who discovers when the historical situation permits an alternate path of development, a creative step in a new direction. New situations arise constantly and demand novel, unstereotyped responses. The leader is a formative force in history. It is true that he is confined by his own time and atmosphere, that his ideas must be in line with the challenges of his generation. But he is not merely passive; he is not only an effect. Events take shape through him, and his own creative ideas become a vital part of the course of history. The question whether a specific challenge will or will not be met is precisely answered by the presence or the absence of the redemptive leader. His concern, clarity of mind, energy of will and creative imagination, his fellowship with God, and desire to serve man will make the total difference.

Perhaps we could make Paul's prayer for the Philippians our own. The substance of his prayer is that "love may abound more and more, with knowledge and all discernment, so that you may approve what is excellent, and may be pure and blameless for the day of Christ, filled with the fruits of righteousness which come through Jesus Christ, to the glory and praise of God" (Phil. 1:9-11).

A prayer for the heart: Love exists, but the apostle prays that it may abound. We love God but because he first loved us. The foundation of love is in God; our love is merely a response. Love is an exotic plant transplanted from God to us. Paul prays for abundant love, but within the bounds of good sense and discretion. Love grows gradually—more and more. Paul is not asking for magic but for normal growth. Love should grow in knowledge. Love and knowledge are inseparable. Knowledge of God is gained through communion; the knowledge of others through experience; the knowledge of truth through meditation on the Word of God.

Love must also abound in discernment, in spiritual insight and feeling, in moral tact. Love imparts sensitivity, keen perception. Paul warns against unregulated impulse, against partiality, against a caricature of love.

A prayer for the mind: Approve what is excellent. The choice is not between good and evil, but between that which is merely good and that which is best. Approve and do the best among all the things that are good. This is a demand for transcendence, for excellence.

A prayer for character: Positively: be pure, sincere, with a single motivation, genuinely open toward God. Negatively: blameless, without offense, not a stumbling block—and all this with an eye on the day of Christ's return. Such a man has perspective, and eschatology becomes meaningful, intersecting with the preoccupations of daily life.

A prayer for life: Filled—the measure—with the fruits of righteousness—a definition of good works. The root, the foundation is Jesus Christ. The realization of this prayer is possible only "through Jesus Christ." The ultimate purpose is the glory and praise of God. When God's character is reflected in the Christian leader, God's glory is seen in man.

Love . . . knowledge . . . discernment . . . excellence . . . righteousness . . . the glory of God: these are a recapitulation of the basic qualities of redemptive Christian leadership.